W9-ADE-988

ALMONTE ONTARIO
K0A 1A0
...LKINSON ST

Channeling - Michael

5/24

Earth to Tao

Michael's Guide

to Healing and Spiritual Growth

•

by Jose Stevens, Ph.D.

Earth to Tao

Michael's Guide to Healing and Spiritual Growth

Copyright c 1989 Jose Luis Stevens
First Printing

Published by:

Affinity Press
2 Austin Court
Orinda, California 94563

All rights reserved. No part of this book may be reproduced or transmitted in any form or by any means, electronic or mechanical, including photocopying, recording or by any information storage and retrieval system without written permission from the publisher, except for the inclusion of brief quotations in a review. Where this information is used for quotation or reference, the author would greatly appreciate being informed in writing.
I am interested in your views and any further information. Please write to P.O. Box 5314, Berkeley, Ca. 94705.

Printed and bound in the United States.
Cover design by Nina Bookbinder.

ISBN 0-942663-03-9
LCCN 89-083785

Dedication

To the important men friends in my life: Ron Drifka, Don Steinert, Jim Reed, Greg Sinclair, and Carlos Stevens.

Acknowledgments

I want to express my appreciation for everyone who contributed in their way to this book:

You the reader for imagining this book.

Michael for the teachings.

All the channels for their time and energy: Lena and Jose Stevens; Larry Keveson; JP Van Hulle; Aaron Christeaan.

Nina Bookbinder for her cover design.

Anna and Carlos for their patience and understanding.

Lenore Schuh for illustrations.

Denise Alpern for graphics, layout, and formatting.

A Brief Overview

The goal of this body of knowledge is to promote unconditional acceptance of self and others. Of course should you find this a challenge, mild tolerance will suffice to start with.

This knowledge is being re-introduced, as it has been historically during times of great change, to help with the current planetary shift toward the mature soul stage. The people of Earth have been dominated for thousands of years by young soul lessons and play. They have amassed power, wealth, influence, and glory. Now the majority are ready to grow to a new level of perception. The new mature level of perception focuses on the value of relationships and growth through self understanding.

Although this teaching is not associated with any currently known philosophy, psychology, or religion, readers will recognize elements of many systems of thought, both Eastern and Western. Perhaps the most recognizable are the works of Gurdjieff and his students Ouspensky and Rodney Collin, pioneers who began disseminating this knowledge earlier in this century.

More recently, this system of knowledge has been channeled by a variety of competent students who are dedicated to the twin values of self understanding and unconditional acceptance of others.

Michael, the non-physical source of this information, gives it freely and unconditionally to anyone who is interested. Michael is simply a convenient name for an experienced entity who once lived many lifetimes upon the earth. Michael completed the lessons and games of the physical plane and now compassionately teaches from experience.

Contents

PART TWO RELATING TO THE PLANET

PART THREE HEALING AND BALANCE

Preface

The source of the material in this book is Michael as well as the psyches of the various channels who worked together to access this body of knowledge. A channel is a person who is able to access wisdom from a non-physical source and deliver it accurately through speech, automatic writing, or other technique.

Nevertheless, any channeled information is subject to distortion by the personality of the channel, the time of day, weather factors, and a great number of other variables. By using more than one channel, I was able to cross-check and keep the information consistent throughout. Since most channeled information is a one man or woman operation, this is not usually possible. Michael is unique in that he is glad to come through a great variety of talented channels. This keeps the teaching fresh, consistent, and non-exclusive.

Michael has always insisted that you validate all channeled information for yourself. This is the only way to truly learn and grow. Therefore do not believe anything you read here. Simply check it out for yourself.

One of my tasks as the author was to organize, edit, and transcribe tapes of channeled material from evening talks and notes from private sessions. This represented years worth of channeled material. My other principal task was to channel information to fill the gaps in the material and create bridges between parts that were isolated from one another. Therefore I wrote much of this book in a light trance state.

The book is divided into four parts so that you can readily find major subject areas. If you wish, you can read the book from cover to cover, or you can use it as a reference, looking up areas of interest as you will.

Introduction

This book builds upon the foundation set down in "The Michael Handbook: A Channeled System for Self Understanding" and "Tao to Earth: Michael's Guide to Relationships and Growth". "The Michael Handbook" details the fascinating relationship between essence and personality and describes at length all the facets that make up personality, lifetime after lifetime. It covers soul age development and describes current and coming global transformation in terms of essence development planet-wide. "Tao to Earth" went on to describe a fascinating array of interpersonal and intrapersonal relationships and how they help to further personal and planetary growth.

Here in this book you will discover how to work with all this knowledge in order to heal yourself and find balance. You will become acquainted with some of the major tools of the planet and learn how to use these tools for maximum benefit. As always, Michael gives you rich and specific explanations of processes and systems that have heretofore been poorly understood, with some surprises thrown in for good measure. As Michael frequently says, "This represents the tiniest fraction of all there is to know. All you have to do to obtain it is to ask."

For those of you who may wish to refresh your memory or become acquainted with the Michael System for the first time, I have included a brief review of the basic teachings in appendix A. Reading this section will help tremendously in understanding the concepts upon which this book is based.

PART ONE

SPIRITUALITY

Chapter One

Awakening and Enlightenment

The Tao (or God) thinking aloud.

    Those parts of myself that I tossed out there to find their way back, sure do seem lost. I guess its time to remind them about some of the signposts and tools that I cached along the trail. I'm excited about their return because they have learned so much and helped me create so much since they agreed to go explore my kingdoms. Guess they've been having some real adventures. They sure do have a knack for suffering though. That wasn't my original idea, but they thought it was a good idea, so, who am I to stop them. We'll have such a good reunion when they remember where they came from and they recall who they are. Well, I guess I did agree to give them all the time they need. But then, what's time to me? I guess I can afford to wait. They look pretty lost, but with a little help they'll be coming around soon enough. I better get the party things out, you never know just how quickly they'll find out and be here. I'd hate to be caught napping.

SPIRITUAL TRADITIONS AND RELIGION

Many of the concepts of spirituality that are presented here can be found embodied in the mystery schools of world religions and in the "perennial philosophy," as Theosophy is called. Whereas in the West many of the concepts have been split among religion, science, and philosophy, in the East these concepts are more integrated in the great Eastern religions. None of these religions, however, portray the Logos accurately. In fact, as a whole they carry major distortions and are misleading in fundamental ways. Nevertheless millions of fragments have been able to struggle through the maze of confusion and reach insight into the nature of the Tao.

The richness, depth, and comprehension of true spirituality is not readily apparent from the recent traditional western viewpoint. Nevertheless, the importance of presence, wakefulness, discipline, emotional and intellectual balance, and energetic practices can be found in the spiritual traditions of every continent in the world. These basic and underlying notions of spiritual development unify the northern and southern hemispheres and the eastern and western regions of the globe.

For example, the basic notion of the chakras as energy centers, vital to well-being and health, can be found cross-culturally in ancient texts. Chakras have been examined and described by the Tibetan Buddhists, by the Hopi tribe of America, as well as African and Siberian shamanic cultures. Certainly the understanding of karma, the law of cause and effect, is a fundamental tenet of Buddhism, Hinduism, Mohammedism, and Christianity as well.

THE CONTEXT OF THIS TEACHING

The notions of the spiritual path are widespread throughout the mystery schools of the major religions, such as the Qabbalists, Essenes, and Sufis. Sufism itself is strongly aligned with the concepts and goal of being awake and pursuing your spiritual path. It too seeks to offer concepts and insights on how this journey may be undertaken. In fact, Sufism was the base for the teachings of Georges Gurdjieff, a fragment who channeled much of the foundation for this teaching.

The early vehicle of many of the concepts and practices discussed here can be found in the shamanic tradition, the root of all religions. In ancient times a form of superstitious shamanism formed the context for the infant soul's expression and under-standing of spirituality. Gradually as the planet entered a new era of baby soul perceptivity, shamanism was suppressed in favor of highly organized and hierarchical religions that structured spirituality for the masses. Religion was created and practiced according to complex laws.

Over time as young souls began to predominate, many of the perennial truths became distorted, clouded, and forgotten because of political maneuvering and the overall loss of clarity regarding the original concepts. From time to time transcendental souls and the infinite soul made appearances to restate the original truths and remind humanity about its relationship to the Tao. With each appearance however the truths were interpreted according to the understanding of the prevailing soul perceptivity, baby and young.

As the population on earth matured and mature souls made their appearance, mystery schools began to appear within the popular religions. These were considered highly suspect but were tolerated if they remained underground or kept a low profile. They were persecuted or wiped out if they were too open about their activities. This has been the case until quite recently when with the emergence of more mature and old souls, teachings such as this one have come forth with more and more frequency. The surfacing of more personal forms of spiritual practice paradoxically brings back a resurgence of shamanism without its early superstitious notions.

The concepts presented in this book, then, are not new. They have been restated and reformulated in the English language and updated with modern day examples to show their validity and application. They are meant to enhance and support individual spiritual development and practice. They do not in any fashion purport to create another religion.

INTRODUCING SPIRITUALITY

This section on spiritual practices ties together the body of knowledge presented thus far. Here it is integrated, and a context is created for the practical application of this knowledge.

The spiritual practices section provides tools for improving life experience and getting more satisfaction out of living. Here you can learn to master the art of living through understanding the underlying concepts and processes of conscious transformation.

The tools provided in this section enable you to handle all the spheres of the physical plane, with its emotional, intellectual, and moving components. With regard to the emotional sphere, you can learn to be open emotionally without being taken advantage of or shutting down at the slightest perceived threat. Intellectually you can learn to live in the knowledge of what is true and still know that you are fallible and will at times choose not to follow your own truth. This means also that you can forgive yourself and return to focus on your truth, managing to keep that balance between truth and falsehood as well as you can. Finally you can learn the art of right action, the ability to move effortlessly and in harmony with the dance of the Tao.

Remember that the aim or the purpose of the game of life is to gradually remember the return to the Tao. In other words, you arrive each lifetime with a basic plan and the purpose of the lifetime is to fulfill that plan and to go through all the experiences and development that you have set up for yourself. This section is aimed at helping you get a picture of the way your basic plan is unfolding. Here some tools are provided so that you may sail and navigate through this plan with a minimum of discomfort, making the most of the enjoyment available to you in the process.

THE SPIRITUAL PERSON

The hallmark of a spiritual person is awareness or the ability to be awake. Being awake requires focus, that is, the ability to be present and focused in physical reality while simultaneously being aware of essence and the other planes of consciousness. Outlined in this chapter are a number of goals or aims of being more awake.

Wakefulness is an essence activity whereas being asleep is a basic function of false personality. Metaphorically speaking, being asleep refers to the act of going through life automatically and mechanically without self-awareness and without examining choices.

You may pour effort and determination into making great amounts of money or climbing to a position of great power in your profession. You can achieve this and still remain asleep because you are driven by false personality goals to survive at all costs, an automatic and mechanical process. On the other hand you can carry out these same activities with the awareness that on an essence level you are seeking challenges that can increase personal integrity and further spiritual growth. Money and power can be neutral vehicles for essence development.

Here are seven aims of being more awake followed by a section on methods to accomplish them.

SEVEN AIMS OF WAKEFULNESS

What does it mean to be more awake and why is it worth the effort?

First wakefulness has to do with being more grounded and aware of the physical body. Awareness of the body allows you to be present. As mentioned earlier, being present is a first step toward being more powerful. Being more powerful allows you to be more in charge of your life and less victimized.

Secondly, being more awake is a product of wider and deeper perception of your own actions and those of others. As you become more perceptive, so do you become more aware of essence directed activity. You learn to stop resisting and live life more effortlessly. Wider perceptivity allows you to become more tolerant of others as you begin to sense their chosen lessons and goals this lifetime. These may be different from your own but just as valid.

Here are seven aims of being more awake.

1.   To act your true soul age.

2.   To disidentify.

3.   To take risks.

4.   To integrate personality and essence.

5.   To remember the Tao.

6.   To attain balance.

7.   To be effective.

DISCUSSION OF AIMS

1. The principal aim of wakefulness is to develop the ability to act from your appropriate soul age be it young, mature, or old. When you consciously act your soul age you automatically begin to move forward in spiritual development.

2. Being awake makes it possible to disidentify from experiences, whether they are pleasurable or painful. Older souls are quite capable of seeing the big picture, which prevents them from becoming too identified with the drama and maya of life.

3. Wakefulness makes it possible to take risks, break through personal limitations, and enjoy taking on challenges. Living on the edge of uncertainty sharpens the senses, promotes alertness, and helps one pay attention to experiences. Living on the edge of uncertainty can also feel most uncomfortable.

> *Perhaps you decide to quit your unsatisfying job in favor of starting a long dreamed-of business. This may involve a true struggle for financial survival. On the other hand you may decide to leave an inappropriate or abusive relationship to live on your own. Those types of experiences often come with the move out of sleep into awareness.*

4. A major aim of being more awake is integrating personality and essence, letting the light of essence shine through personality. When personality integrates with essence you become responsible for your life. Wakefulness provides the possibility of taking an active role in making choices and controlling the outcome of situations in life. Experiences then cease to be random and chaotic and become purposeful essence activity.

Wakefulness, then, allows you to be at cause rather than at the effect of life or a victim of circumstance. The aphorism that "there are no accidents in the universe" encourages wakefulness and awareness of the truth that there is a plan to the universe.

> *The loss of a job or a mate, while perceived as a tragedy by personality alone, can be seen as an opportunity to release undeveloped resources by integrated personality and essence.*

5. Wakefulness facilitates remembering, and remembering furthers the desire to achieve union with the Tao. Wakefulness leads you to discover your own life's purpose, your role in essence, and your life task. These are all functions of remembering who you are in the present, remembering who you have been in past lives, and remembering who you will be when you know your place within the Tao. In each lifetime this provides meaning and substance for the awake human being.

6. An overall goal of becoming more awake is to regain the ability to retain balance in all the centers—instinctive, emotional, intellectual, and moving. In order to become more awake one needs to balance lower centers and through this balance reach the higher centers—the higher emotional, intellectual, and moving centers—via the instinctive center.

> *When you are paying attention you are more likely to feel, think, and act simultaneously. From this balanced point of power you neutralize your fears and experience insight, relatedness, and beauty. Imagine the joy of skiing gracefully and rapidly, an activity requiring absolute attention.*

7. Wakefulness is desirable because the state of being unaware and asleep is both inconvenient and can lead to embarrassment.

When you are not paying attention you walk into walls, crash your car, and put your shoes into the refrigerator. Psychologically and spiritually speaking when you go unconscious you may feel driven, lose direction, and create negative karma.

In summary, being on the physical plane calls for having a personality. Having a personality is accompanied by forgetfulness of wholeness, a kind of spiritual amnesia. To make matters more interesting this amnesia includes a forgetfulness that you are asleep and ignorance of the fact that there is anything to remember.

So you can walk around thinking you are awake when you are actually dreaming. You may actually think it is normal to feel depressed or angry all the time.

The challenge here is to hold the contradiction that it is necessary to be asleep in order to move to being awake. Therefore in some lifetimes the seeking out of new experiences is more important than being awake. Being asleep is then a necessary experience to explore. The overall goal of remaining awake predominates.

BALANCING THE CENTERS

Intentional awakening is fostered by the perception that one has not achieved one's potential. In order to reach higher levels of awareness (higher centers) or what your late Western psychologist Abraham Maslow has termed "peak experiences," three conditions are necessary. These conditions are: a powerful desire to know the truth; a willingness to be emotionally open to life; and a practiced ability to be balanced energetically.

How is this done? First of all it is important to realize that the higher centers need not be developed. Higher emotional, intellectual, and moving centers are already developed.

The higher centers are like a bicycle, completely intact, sitting in the closet waiting for the child to develop enough coordination and skill to use it.

The task is to access these higher centers through the balance of the lower centers; intellectual, emotional and moving.

Intellectual, emotional, and moving centers form a triad which relate to the universal building blocks truth, love, and energy, a triad that relates in turn to the three axes on the overleaf chart; expression, inspiration, and action.

By balancing the lower centers one is then able to balance and integrate all that is represented on the overleaf chart.

The following are methods which can promote the balance of these three lower centers. Afterwards we will discuss the role of the instinctive center and methods to work with it.

INTELLECTUAL CENTER
Being able to tell the truth intellectually to oneself and to others
Being aware of one's goal in life
Perceiving and understanding one's issues and fears
Acting from essence or from the positive pole of one's attitude
Holding the neutral perspective
Observing the way the universe works and one's position in it
Developing the ability to study appropriately

EMOTIONAL CENTER
Being aware of self and others in the big picture
Practicing perceptivity and learning to trust it
Demonstrating compassion towards self and others
Enlisting support from and supporting others
Achieving balance by clearing emotional blocks
Practicing unconditional self-acceptance
Seeing oneself and others as perfect the way they are

MOVING CENTER
Right action (a Buddhist term meaning having integrity in all actions)
Fulfilling agreements, including a commitment to one's own goals
Taking responsibility for one's actions
Striving for conscious completion of octaves and karma
Organizing what needs to be done without creating stress
Placing intention on the ability to carry through
Eliminating mechanical behavior and deadening habits
Erasing the chief feature and being aware of false personality
Practicing meditation and concentration
Mastering the use of the physical body, which includes diet, exercise, and sexuality
Finding the balancing point of the polarities in one's personal overleaf configuration

A final note: consciousness can still exist with or without balanced centers. For example you may be conscious even if you are spiritually still asleep. The trick is to be not only conscious but aware of your experience at the same time. This is not the same as being self-conscious in the psychological sense, a condition that is born of the chief feature of arrogance.

When you are dancing and you think about your feet you are likely to trip. If you worry about how silly you look you will not enjoy yourself and will not dance well. You may be conscious but are not aware that you are forgetting the overall experience of the dance. Awareness of all centers at once creates the harmony and pleasure of the dance.

SEVEN STEPS TO SELF-AGAPE

Remember that the goal of this teaching is to facilitate the lessons of unconditional love and acceptance. There is no possibility of accomplishing this toward others if you have not first learned how to unconditionally accept yourself. Here are seven steps to lead you in that direction.

1. Trust in your perceptivity.

2. Ruthless truthfulness with yourself.

3. Acknowledging that the world and those in it are perfect and making a commitment to be tolerant.

4. Allow yourself your own power and constant choice to be appropriate with it.

5. Erasing fear and the chief negative feature to live in gentleness and joy.

6. Truly experiencing surrender and therefore power and control, which leads to the true integration of personality and essence. This allows you to fully experience the physical plane as well as the truth, love, and beauty of the other planes.

7. Humility.

1. Trust in your perceptivity.

The first step to self-agape has to do with developing your ability to perceive. Perceiving is not thinking about, nor is it figuring out or scrutinizing. Remember that perceptivity is a function of your emotional center and that perception is a feeling. This is the ability to size up the truth of a situation, experience, or person by instantly and emotionally sensing what is so about them.

> *You might walk into a business meeting where a number of people are present and you can instantly perceive whom you can trust and whom you should be careful about. You can instantly perceive as well whether you are going to get anywhere with this team or whether you are going to waste time and money with them.*

The aphorism "Don't guess, perceive," applies to this step. This is an important way to look at perceptivity. Your society does not encourage people to follow and trust their own intuitions and perceptions. Characteristically older souls, because of their experience, have inherently good perceptivity skills. The problem tends to be that older souls lose confidence in their perceptivity when they live in a young soul society that places a low value on intuition and perception. Thus, this first step to self-agape is to trust and develop the skill of perception.

2. Ruthless truthfulness with yourself.

The second step to self-agape encourages you to be completely honest with yourself. Ruthless truthfulness means the courage to state what is so about yourself and your perceptions at any one time. This truthfulness does not have so much to do with perceiving as it does with telling the truth about what you perceived. Often you perceive accurately but then deny what you saw, or distort is so much that the truth becomes unrecognizable.

You may accurately assess that the business team gathered is a bad mix of personalities and that your endeavors will come to grief. However, if you should slide to the negative poles of your overleaves and become, for example, ingratiating, you may deny to yourself and the others your original perception. You will act as if everything is fine and proceed foolishly into a mess.

Knowing and telling the truth, however, can be tricky. Because the truth is unique for each individual, one person's truth is another person's lie. In addition, truth is not always constant but changes as the soul matures and gains experience. The truth for a baby soul is different from the truth for a mature soul. The truth for a baby soul is that law, order, and obedience to authority are the most necessary ingredients to live a good life. The truth for a mature soul is that individual search and questioning of authority is necessary for a good life.

Ruthless truthfulness is a form of compassion and need not be seen as a way of putting oneself down or being self-deprecating. Being self-truthful is not beating yourself up but seeing in a detached way what the reality is and what must be done.

3. Acknowledging that the world and the people in it are perfect and making a commitment to be tolerant.

The third step focuses on acknowledging that people are perfect the way they are. Perfect means that each person is following his or her own path just the way that they should. In other words, every person is learning their lessons in his or her chosen ways. The important lesson one person is learning may be the important lesson that another person learned ten lifetimes ago or will learn three lifetimes from now.

Therefore perfection does not have to be a high ideal or look like your pictures of what the world is supposed to be, but in fact what is.

The concept of perfection in what is has always been one of the most difficult for students to understand. You may ask, how can the world be perfect if there is killing, war, famine, and disease? How can so-and-so be perfect if he lies, cheats, and steals from me? Should I do nothing, then, to correct or stop these things? The answer is paradoxical. Yes, all these things are being perfectly done and everyone is learning their lessons exactly the way they had hoped (on an essence level, of course). However, part of this perfection is that when you perceive injustice you perfectly move to correct it. Therefore physical reality is a game that everyone gets to play, the unjust and the just, and in the illusion of time one will eventually become the other, and the game continues.

4. Allow yourself your own power and the constant choice to be appropriate with it.

Personal power is the result of telling the truth. Telling the truth gives you presence, and presence is perceived as power. Being appropriate with power is a unique task for each individual.

The more powerful a person is, the simpler the message. The philosophical writings of young souls are often lengthy, complex, and difficult to read. The message of old souls tends to be far simpler. The teachings and concepts of Jesus Christ are immensely powerful and are phrased in the simplest possible terms, as in the parables and in statements such as "Love your neighbor as yourself." The Buddha taught the eightfold path based on the simple truth that to crave is to suffer. Meher Baba said, "Don't worry, be happy." What could be simpler?

5. Erase fear and your chief negative feature to live in gentleness and joy.

Attention and awareness are the chief tools for erasing fear. Fear is a by-product of the false personality and when you shift your identification away from the false personality and toward essence you automatically begin to dissolve fear.

All seven chief features—self-destruction, greed, self-depre-cation, arrogance, martyrdom, impatience, and stubbornness—are based on fears. A major life task each lifetime is to erase the neutralizing effect of the chief feature so that you can reach your goal. When you are realizing your life goal, whether it is acceptance or growth, you feel the joy of essence work. The experience of joy always leads to gentleness.

6. *Truly experiencing surrender and therefore power and control. This allows you to fully experience the physical plane as well as the truth, love, and beauty of the other planes.*

As you can see, step six contains a paradox, calling on you to experience surrender while at the same time experiencing personal power. You need to be able to hold this contradiction at one and the same time in order to be in control.

In one sense surrender means no longer resisting the events and experiences of the physical plane. Surrender does not mean giving up, but embracing essence-directed lessons and opportunities. When you stop resisting being in a body and the karma that accompanies it, you begin to rapidly accelerate your spiritual growth. As you accelerate you become more powerful because you learn to fear nothing.

Spiritual growth allows you to access the higher centers—higher intellectual, higher emotional, and higher moving. As you begin to open up to the higher centers you begin to experience the truth, love, and beauty of all the planes within the Tao.

7. *Humility*

This seventh step is the experience of completion after you have mastered the first six steps. The seventh step allows you to let go of attachment to that achievement and this neutrality is expressed as humility.

ENLIGHTENMENT

What is enlightenment and is it attainable?

To put it simply, enlightenment is a single experience in a higher center. Enlightenment is not a constant state which can be lived in on the physical plane. Nor is enlightenment something which, contrary to popular opinion, once experienced, remains with you forever. Nevertheless, enlightenment is attainable. Enlightenment is also losable. How can this be? Lets take a look.

The experience of enlightenment can come about through any situation or event. For example enlightenment can occur while you are eating your broccoli, brushing your teeth, or driving down the highway. Usually however, these tasks are experienced as mundane and are done automatically. You can, however, push through the mundanity of these acts and experience enlightenment doing them.

Enlightenment is actually a product of the triad, truth, love, and energy. These, as you will remember, are accessed through the higher intellectual center, higher emotional center, and higher moving center. The truth is perceived; love is experienced; and energy provides integration which lights up higher experience. We call this en-light-enment. Enlightenment is a sensed or felt energetic connectedness that is built on the experience of truth and love.

Imagine you are occupied with the mundane task of driving your car down a busy section of highway. Normally you might be bored and let your focus drift to past events or future worries. However this time you are energetically and vitally aware of yourself as alive and present in the act of driving. You perceive the truth of your relatedness to the Tao and experience a pervasive sense of love for yourself and everything around you. You become lighter or enlightened for a moment.

So enlightening moments can be experienced and the memory of the enlightening experiences can help you to reexperience or reachieve the enlightened state.

Enlightenment is an intensely personal event in that only you know when you have experienced it. Most individuals are so moved by the experience that they decide to share it as best they can.

There are myriad forms and degrees of enlightenment because each person occupies a different place on the path of development. Your movement in this developmental schema is unique and comprises a series of incremental steps. Because of this, if you are devoted to your own spiritual development and wish to move toward enlightenment, you can have experiences that are partial glimpses of your true origins. You may sense on an intuitive level your connectedness or perhaps see the intuitive overview of the purpose of your lifetime.

> *If you are first level mature you may have an enlightened glimpse at your greater relatedness to your neighbors and friends. If you are seventh level old you may have an enlightened perception of your imminent experience of cycling off to join your entity.*

Western society does not foster or encourage the notions of perceptivity or enlightenment. Conditioning and programming can shut down the motivation to seek enlightenment up to a point. However eventually the urge surfaces no matter what the general beliefs of the culture are. You can focus your experiences and perceptions and with practice and support develop to a point where the experience is more and more attainable.

Many spiritual traditions emphasize the importance of attaining enlightenment as a goal and persuade people to orient their entire lives towards achieving this experience. Since enlightenment as a goal is placed out into the future, it tends to move you away from awareness of the moment. Therefore, enlightenment is better considered as a by-product of experience rather than a specific goal towards which you work .

The goal of being on the physical plane is to experience the physical plane and not necessarily remove oneself from it. Therefore enlightenment is best seen as a place to visit and not as a place to live.

Historically some individuals have sought a life of austerity and total isolation in order to reach a state of enlightenment.

Some individuals have lived in Himalayan caves in order to remain in the higher centers and experience enlightenment. Others have closed themselves up in cloisters or monasteries to concentrate on satori or nirvana. Still others have roamed the land as beggars hoping for higher centered experiences.

This system does not hold that cutting yourself off from the rigors and pleasures of everyday life is in fact successfully handling the physical plane. However, a life of privacy and isolation is appropriate for some individuals who have specific goals in mind. This type of life is not useful spiritually speaking should it be sought out as an escape from modern society.

This system holds that the purpose of life is to master the physical plane and this means achieving your own concepts or goals of success including spiritual achievement within the context of everyday life.

In other words you are actually addressing being a person in a body on the physical plane when you are handling the issues of a job, children and the ordinary demands of day-to-day life.

In summary then, enlightenment is a state reached through the higher centers. It is a temporary condition and is experienced by degree; that is each person will experience it according to their own capacity.

You have seen the importance of staying awake when you are interested in accelerated spiritual evolution. You have also learned the importance of balancing the centers in your quest for higher degrees of enlightenment. You know the value of unconditionally accepting yourself and the steps to bring you closer to that goal. Now, in this next section we will focus on the degrees of essence and how you can be aware of them.

DEGREES OF ESSENCE

How do you recognize essence within you? How does essence manifest in the various soul levels? What is the nature of essence and the physical body's relationship with it?

Here we will discuss the relationship that you have with your own essence—yourself. Now while you occupy a physical body here on earth your personality tends to be heavily focused in only one plane of existence. However, the truth is that all planes exist simultaneously and your essence lives in all of them at once. So you have a curious situation in which your personality is consciously aware of your daily routine here while you as an essence are touching base with all realities at the same moment. You are more or less aware of your essence activities depending on your soul development, your cultural imprinting, and your overleaves.

So, you might say that you are aware of degrees of essence activity in each lifetime. Generally speaking the older your soul level the more degrees of essence you are aware of. Remember that because of special circumstances this may not always be true. You may be an older soul with difficult karma or overleaves that tend to shut off your awareness. Or you may be a younger soul with overleaves and cultural imprinting that cause you to accelerate your awareness level.

Let us here elucidate the seven degrees of essence and discuss the nature of each.

First Degree of Essence

In the first degree of essence you are aware of yourself as a fragment, a physical body with personality overleaves. You are aware of how your physical body works, how to take care of it, and how to clothe and feed it. You are aware of your major lessons and monads (relationships). You experience time as linear and sequential and the events of the physical plane seem totally real to you. You often act out of the negative poles of your overleaves and false personality is in control. Death appears to be ever-lurking and final. Fear is prevalent.

At this degree of essence you are focused on what separates you from everything else. This is the most isolated, lonely, and contracted awareness level. Even though this degree of essence is characteristic of infant and baby souls, all soul levels are capable of acting out of this degree if stressed.

Second Degree of Essence

At the second degree of essence you experience your over-leaves in the positive poles and you are deeply aware of your role in essence. Here you learn about essence relationships such as essence twins and many of your monads. You become aware of major quadrants or sextants that you participate in as well as your support group.

Here essence learns the mechanics of how it relates to other essences. Past lives are remembered and underlying themes that include prior lifetimes come to awareness. Time is suspended more often and being is considered as important as doing. Activities on the astral plane are recalled such as out-of-body experiences and lucid dreams.

Third Degree of Essence

The third degree of essence is characterized by awareness of your entity mates and your cadre. You become aware of your relationships with others from a past-present-future context. You are aware of past life connections as well as probable future ones. You are able to recognize essence twins from past cycles and relationships have a deep familiarity to them.

Here you become aware of the fact that you are living as well in parallel universes. Your awareness is thus more expansive and more pervasive. On occasion, under optimal conditions, young souls can achieve this degree of essence.

Fourth Degree of Essence

The fourth degree of essence is the neutral zone represented by instinctive center awareness. Since your instinctive center houses all the mechanical memory of how to survive, knowledge that you have gained over past lives, you become acutely aware of these programs. You are able to weather the fear and struggle that accompanies dropping old patterns of survival, a little like the butterfly shedding its cocoon.

Here you become capable of remembering probable futures that you have planned for yourself. This shows up as skill in precognition or déjà vu. You are also able to actively work with your own parallel universes, making constructive contact with them and consciously bringing over useful information from them.

Fifth Degree of Essence

At the fifth degree of essence you gain active knowledge of parallel universes and what laws exist in each of them. You are able to sense your connections with yourself in those parallel existences and can gain support from your relationships and experiences there as well as here.

Here you begin to experience others as yourself and agape is the result. This is most typically true for members of your own entity whose life experiences begin to feel like your own. If an entity mate is struggling with an intense issue you are aware of it and realize that its positive resolution will heal you as well.

The fifth degree of essence is related to higher intellectual awareness.

Sixth Degree of Essence

The sixth degree of essence is characterized by an awareness of your entity's relationship with other entities. You are able to recognize people that belong to entities that you often relate to. For example you may recognize a member of your best friend's entity as you are shopping in the market. You are able to recognize the energy as being similar.

You become aware of relationships that are not physical and experience the joy at knowing them as well as the loneliness at missing them. You are aware of your connectedness with them even though they seem to be very far away. Your relationship with them often becomes noticeable in dream activity.

The sixth degree of essence is related to higher emotional awareness.

Seventh Degree of Essence

At the seventh degree of essence you experience your connectedness with all that is. This is a grounded state of being in which you are able to function completely adequately in the world, while at the same time you feel the infiniteness of your being.

You are aware of your connectedness with the planet and all its lifeforms. You are aware of your relationship to all the physical universe as well as the non-physical universe. You feel your connection to all parallel universes and acknowledge your experiences there.

You are able to manifest at all levels of your being at once.

The seventh degree of essence is related to the higher moving center.

All degrees of essence co-exist at the same time. All are available to tap into at any given moment. However, as mentioned, here on the physical plane you tend to shut out many of these degrees of essence to concentrate and focus on specific lessons and experiences. A master is one who is experienced and has chosen to be aware of all seven levels at once.

Now let us look at the chief obstacles that block spiritual awareness and keep you from remembering who you truly are. Let us turn to the subject of maya.

Chapter Two

Illusions

MAYA

Maya is an ancient Sanskrit term meaning illusion. Everything on the physical plane is maya; the physical body, your personality each lifetime, all of the overleaves, and even solid matter around you. Maya especially refers to those experiences stemming from the negative poles of the overleaves.

Maya is very much like watching a movie. The movie appears real but is actually a series of single-frame still pictures moving rapidly on a screen. These still frames were recorded at an earlier date. The illusion is that there is action happening right now in front of you. You are made to believe that the heroine is actually being carried away by the giant gorilla. The physical

*plane is like the most real movie you have ever seen. You
are mesmerized by it and believe that every minute of it
is real.*

Maya is essentially a lie. The Tao allows maya to exist
within itself so that it can play the great game. When you play
chess or checkers or Monopoly you must believe it is a real-life
challenge in order to exercise your skills and have fun. So maya is
like a veil that makes it easier for you to believe the game you
are involved in. This hones your living skills and allows you to
enter the drama of it all. Through it the Tao can challenge itself.

Therefore maya exists for a reason. Maya is not bad, but it
certainly is something to eventually see through.

THE MAYA OF EACH SOUL LEVEL

Now, the earlier the soul level the more obvious or basic the
maya. Maya becomes much more subtle with the older soul levels. For example a baby soul may believe arrogantly that he is
the most important person around and is better than other people.
This is a form of maya. An old soul may believe that because he
meditates and practices yoga he is somehow spiritually more
aware than others. This is a more subtle form of maya. The
further along the spiritual path one progresses, the more tricky
and deceptive is the maya. Let us examine for a moment the
maya inherent in each soul level.

The Maya of The Infant Soul

The infant soul has entered the first stage of the human cycle
in the game of life. The infant soul retains the fearfulness and
survival orientation that characterized its experiences in the
earlier plant, insect, and animal kingdoms. Infant souls quickly
lose contact with the Tao and enter the maya of maximum
separateness and most fearfulness. The infant soul truly believes

MAYA

he is isolated and he resists enculturation in favor of survival at a sustenance level. Lacking a developed sense of identity he may have trouble knowing his own boundaries.

> *Think of a newborn whose mother leaves the room. As an adult you can see that mother has just stepped out the door to answer the phone. But to the newborn, mother has just disappeared from the face of the earth.*

The first step in the infant soul's challenge to maya is learning to cooperate with others and learning to live with a sense of order and structure.

The Maya of the Baby Soul

The baby soul believes that if only society and civilization were more structured, and if only everybody obeyed god or authority according to the rules and regulations, everything would be fine. At first this sort of lesson is valuable for baby souls because it eases the chaos of the infant soul maya.

> *The belief that if you are good, you will go to heaven, and if bad you will go to hell, definitely acts as a strong deterrent to the maya of senseless brutality.*

This form of maya tends to limit individual expression and promotes a rigid hierarchical social structure that makes the baby soul feel safe. Within this belief system the needs of others are not considered individually but only in the mass. Heretics can easily burn at the stake for stepping outside the system. So, you can see that the inherent benefits of the baby soul lessons can also lead to intense maya. Therefore the baby soul is pushed toward new lessons that diminish maya even further.

Baby souls eventually need to learn to honor and respect individuality in self and in others.

The Maya of The Young Soul

Young souls have learned to see themselves and others as unique human beings. They have begun to learn to search out their own expression of who they are. However they quickly become snagged by social pressure and cultural belief systems. They fall into the trap of believing that if they just had the appropriate goods and social standing everything would be fine. The motivation to achieve these can turn into a burning desire, leading them to regard others as enemies who stand in the way of what they want. So, the circle of maya continues.

Because the drive to achieve and amass material power and wealth becomes so prominent the young soul may neglect emotional and spiritual development.

Here we have the next set of lessons that erodes the maya of the young soul. He needs to learn to honor emotions and experience the value of true spiritual insight.

The Maya of The Mature Soul

The mature soul turns inward away from the intense competition of the young soul cycle. He becomes deeply emotional and begins to pose existential questions about the nature of his being. He becomes a seeker, and quickly disposes of the maya inherent in the young soul era. However this is only to be replaced with a more subtle form of maya. The mature soul begins to believe that he should be able to understand himself completely as well as understand everyone else. He also believes that he should be understood by others. This expectation is a wish to be understood emotionally as well as intellectually. This leads him into intense feelings of victimization and self doubt when understanding is not forthcoming. This is again a state of heavy maya.

Furthermore the mature soul becomes subject to intense idealism, believing that there should be equity for all, as in an ideal socialistic state and that everyone should want peace and harmony. This of course is a reaction to the me-ism and self orientation of the young soul cycle and again this carries with it its very own maya.

In addition mature souls believe that if they delve deeply enough into emotional drama they will achieve clarity and spiritual insight. This often turns into a never-ending series of incomplete scenarios similar in style to the ongoing drama of a television soap opera. This eventually leads the mature soul into an awareness of the next lesson involving maya.

The mature soul needs to learn disidentification. He needs to learn to tell the difference between having emotions and getting lost in them. In short he needs to learn that he is not his emotions. He needs to learn as well that not everyone wants what he wants and that some people prefer inequity and disharmony for experience's sake. Finally he needs to learn patience with regard to understanding.

The Maya of The Old Soul

Old souls by and large have learned a measure of detachment from their emotional drama. They have learned to tolerate the different points of view of others. They have developed the ability to proceed without complete understanding and are aware that they do not know everything.

The old soul is confronted with the most subtle maya of all. He may slip into the illusion that because he has experienced so much over his many lifetimes that he is somehow a better human being than younger souls. Furthermore he may even feel that he has nothing to learn from the younger souls around him.

> *Imagine an old codger executive arrogantly trying to tell younger staff members that he knows better how to do things because he has been around longer. He may feel that these younger workers don't know anything and they should listen to him.*

The old soul, beginning to feel somewhat tired and lazy in his old age, can easily slip into the illusion that the universe owes him a living for all the hard work he has done. However, it does not matter whether he was Cleopatra in his last lifetime, he must still carry his own weight in this new one.

In this vein the old soul can become impatient to complete the experience of the physical plane, feeling that to still be physical is an unnecessary burden. He may moan and groan about it, acting like he is above any more mundane experiences. Or he may feel that spiritual experiences are definitely better than ordinary physical ones (as if there were a difference). As a result he misses out on the potential all around him for even more growth, for if he were truly finished with the physical plane he would not now be in a body.

Old souls can become too detached from their emotions, preferring to be intellectually centered following the intense emotional drama of the mature soul cycle. They may desire to stay aloof from everyday interactions with other people. They can become less than compassionate with their fellows still struggling with emotional issues.

> *Imagine the aloof drill sergeant, grilling his troops in the most difficult exercises. He reasons that if he makes them tough they will survive the rigors of battle. But some of his men fall ill from the exercises. He has forgotten what it is like to be in training himself.*

The old soul may even figure that if he hides out he will not incur any more karma. However resisting karma only increases self-karma. The only solution is to return to the front lines again.

So the old soul has some very significant challenges in the form of subtle maya. He needs to learn patience and unconditional acceptance of his experience. He needs to accept responsibility for full expression each and every lifetime. He needs to learn detachment with participation. Finally he needs to learn how to integrate all of his experiences through a balance of the emotional, intellectual, and moving centers.

The Maya of The Transcendental Soul

Transcendental souls are involved in even more subtle maya. Because they experience themselves as separate identities they are still subject to maya. They still draw distinctions and experience duality.

However the transcendental soul may fall into believing that he knows everything and forget that he also is on a path of remembering. He may accept titles such as "Realized Master" or "Ultimate Authority" given to him by his followers. He may forget that he teaches only one perspective about All That Is.

Infinite Soul

The infinite soul is not involved in maya of any kind. The infinite soul experiences oneness with the Tao and has no separate identity outside the Tao.

THE MAYA OF EACH ROLE

Each role is engaged in its own unique form of maya or illusion. This comes about primarily from acting out of the negative pole of each role. This maya is tricky because each role is blind to its own delusional system; however the inappropriateness is readily seen by others. This is because when you are acting from the negative pole of your role, you tend to affect others more than you affect yourself. The maya of the roles sticks around throughout all the cycles from infant through old. Each lifetime you chip away at it but it has a way of clinging like bubble gum just when you thought you had at last rid yourself of it. Therefore work on cutting through role maya must be relentless and you must develop patience with yourself when you slip back into it.

Let us examine for a moment the maya of each role.

Server: That he is victimized and must serve whether he
likes it or not.
That he always knows best how to serve you,
whether you like it or not.
That he must be in control.
That being out of control is so terrible.
That inspiration is the only thing that is important.

Priest: That he always knows what is good for everyone's
spiritual growth.
That he knows best and doesn't have to think
through or understand thoroughly what he is
talking about.
That what he says and does is always backed up by
ultimate truth or wisdom.
That inspiration is the only thing that is important.
That solid roles are too concrete.

Artisan: That his creations are real.
That the stories he tells himself are based on fact.
That his creations are always wonderful and should
be appreciated by everyone.
That his creations are always novel.
That creating chaos always serves everyone.
That expression is the only thing that is important.
That solid roles are too concrete.

Sage: That everything he has to say is worth listening to.
That everything he has to say is universally true.
That everything should be articulated.
That he is always funny.
That he can only express himself a particular way
(writing, acting, singing).
That expression is the only thing that is important.

Warrior: That might makes right.

That force is effective in dealing with situations.

That retaliation always stops the other side from continuing the fight.

That whatever he is focused on is the only thing worth considering.

That whatever he is focused on is the key to everything.

That taking action is the only way to deal with situations.

That fluid roles are too flaky.

King: That he should always be obeyed.

That he is the one who always knows what is in the best interest of everyone.

That he should always be the leader.

That he is always important and should be noticed.

That overt manipulation is always the best policy.

That action is always the best policy.

That everyone else should want to serve him and wait on him.

Scholar: That his theories are correct.

That the map or model is the same as the territory.

That he knows the facts when actually he is just theorizing.

That neutrality is always the best policy.

That he is always neutral.

That withdrawal in conflict is best.

That analyzing what happened is always useful.

That experiments are always worth doing.

All the negative poles of the overleaves are targets of specific types of maya. The chief features are completely governed by maya. Together these compose the false personality that you eventually cast off. In the next section we will focus on varieties of meditation and spiritual practices that are excellent tools for cutting through maya.

Chapter Three

Tools to Accelerate

MEDITATION

Your day-to-day life is often filled with the frenzy of job schedules, childcare, household chores, and social activities. From morning until night your mind is filled with the thoughts and feelings of daily living.

The function of meditation is to allow, even for a few minutes, the entire human organism to clear all the ongoing chatter so that temporary clarity can be achieved. This has tremendous healing effects on the individual. The Buddhists have aptly named this ongoing mental activity "the drunken monkey mind" because of its way of jumping about from topic to topic, from thought to thought, in an undisciplined, erratic, and compulsive fashion.

This monkey mind chatter is perpetrated by the false personality. The continuous mental activity is geared toward the survival of the organism which is the bastion of the false personality.

The goal or purpose of the false personality is to survive and sustain the belief that it alone is right. The endless chatter of self-talk is in fact a form of self-validation by the false personality. Meditation cuts through the continuous chatter. For this short piece of time you can suspend false personality activity and become aware and attuned to the deeper inner level of essence expression.

Meditation is at first not an easy practice because the false personality is not interested in any practice which results in its defeat.

You may be aware of your own reluctance to practice meditation. You may have made efforts to meditate and found other priorities have crowded out your meditation time. False personality may have quietly gained the upper hand, dictating its own self-serving priorities that increase mental chatter and obscure essence for a time.

On the other hand you may have developed some meditation discipline and have recognized that the more you practice it the stronger essence expression becomes. Why is this so? Meditation furthers the act of remembering at many levels. When the mental chatter ceases, inner knowledge and wisdom are released through direct insight and intuition. Stillness of the mind nourishes "being" rather than "doing," and being in turn opens the way to awareness of essence. Let us look at this process in more depth.

Remember that one of the chief characteristics of meditation is that it quiets and stills the intellectual, emotional, and moving centers. When these lower centers are stilled, the instinctive center opens, releasing its store of fears. The opening of this center can cause considerable discomfort, a process that is discussed in a later section. As you process the survival material in your instinctive center by quietly allowing its release, you begin to open a pathway to the higher centers.

As you enter the higher centers you experience the truth, love, and beauty of the Tao. The isolation and separateness of false personality has been suspended and you experience the relatedness and wholeness of essence.

In some forms of meditation you are encouraged to forget about the body and allow your attention to penetrate into higher planes of existence. When you return your attention to the body, perhaps after a period of hours, you frequently do not remember what has occurred. Meditations that include an awareness of the physical body are recommended because they allow you to re-member and retain the information which has been accessed during the meditation. This is the reason that the Zen master prods and awakens meditators who have nodded off or gone to sleep. This is not a practice of cruelty or punishment as some believe but supports the student in remaining awake.

The practice of meditation encourages the experience of remaining awake and aware in the present and this furthers spiritual development. It also assists one in the enjoyment of everyday life.

Meditation and Soul Age

The practice of meditation is usually pursued by mature and older souls. Younger souls seldom realize or understand the bene-fits of it because they are more oriented to "doing" and perceive meditation as a waste of time.

Most older souls have practiced various forms of meditation over a period of lifetimes. Once a discipline is learned it need not be mastered again and again. The mastery is carried forward to the following lifetimes. Therefore, one person may struggle with meditation for years with few results where an older soul may practice a little meditation with tremendous results. The effects and benefits of meditation are accumulative. The stillness and sense of disidentifying with one's circumstances are enhanced with practice and you can discover the practice of meditation to be an enriching experience.

ADVANCED MEDITATION

You may sit quietly and experience and enjoy the stillness of meditation and be in touch with essence in higher centers. There are, however, advanced techniques for individuals who are heavily committed to spiritual development and who wish to eradicate false personality entirely. This is a substantial task and constitutes "killing off" the false personality, a feat that can be accomplished with great discipline. When the instinctive center opens, great fear may be experienced because the instinctive center also governs the basic survival of the organism. Historically spiritual traditions have warned meditators about the deep fears that can emerge in meditative practice. Occasionally these fears can lead you to believe that you are actually dying. At this point many people quit meditating. This impression or apparent conviction that you are dying is a rite of passage on the path to the ecstasies of the higher centers. You may pass through a brief period of discomfort, only, as mentioned earlier, you carry with you skills and accomplishments learned in prior lifetimes. If you have confronted your demons in one life you will find it easier in the next.

Spiritual traditions throughout the world emphasize the importance of meditation for spiritual development and have stressed the need for support and discipline in its practice. Some disciplines require many years of practice before the person is ready for spiritual insight. All forms of meditation set out to achieve stillness of the mind to promote the perception of inner knowledge and wisdom.

MEDITATION BY AXIS

Priests and Servers

Priests and servers meditate best to music because it is inspirational. Music leads them to a relaxed and more emotional state. It enhances emotional and intellectual inspiration. Music serves them best as a general purpose technique.

This is also true for those with inspirational overleaves such as growth, spiritualism, passion, or emotional centering.

Artisans and Sages

In addition to standard methods of meditation, artisans and sages respond to meditative techniques that utilize sound and words. Chanting, singing hymns, praying, and saying mantras are all effective expression role practices. Monks singing Gregorian chants are in fact practicing a powerful form of meditation.

Visualization and concentration on mock-ups is also helpful to artisans and sages and those with expressive overleaves such as acceptance, idealist, caution, and intellectual centering. Some sages use therapy as a kind of talking meditation and this can work well for them.

Warriors and Kings

The action roles meditate best by not moving. Sitting still, where it is comfortable to relax for the moment without fidgeting around is most effective. As long as they are still, it is not important what other form of meditation they use

When warriors and kings have a sedentary lifestyle, their minds are often actively pursuing single trains of thought without respite. The aim of meditation can be to stop the wheels spinning for just a few minutes. They can back off from the narrow, focused viewpoint and see the broader purpose of what they are doing. They can get inspired and grasp a whole new direction of where they want to go. Zen meditation is excellent for this purpose.

Those with action overleaves such as submission, realist, perseverance, and moving centering respond well to stillness.

Scholars

Scholars can do almost anything to effectively meditate. Scholars and meditation are synonyms. Because scholar is the assimilation role, they live in what other roles would consider to be meditation most of the time.

Those with many neutral overleaves such as flow, pragmatism, and observation will find more flexibility in their meditation practices.

MEDITATION AND THE HIGHER CENTERS

The unfocused purpose of meditation is to relax and let go of the intellectual activity, stand aside from one's feelings and suspend movement. The more you remove the other centers that get in your way, the more you can focus your intent.

As mentioned earlier, when all centers are stilled you enter the instinctive center. This gives your body a chance to deep-breathe for a moment. Then you can move into one of the higher centers.

In the higher intellectual center you can reflect on your own truth. You can clarify where you are and what you want in your life. In the higher emotional center you can be inspired and allow emotional healing to take place. In the higher moving center you can reflect on the beauty of your experience and be aware of refining your energetic field.

At the moment of the higher perceptions you become able to quite literally switch universes. While you are going about your daily business, most of the time you are going around in circles, unaware of the other probabilities and choices available to you. In meditation you back off and look at the big picture.

By looking at the direction you were taking, like an eagle circling above, looking at where it had been walking on the ground, you can see where your path was taking you. Based on this wider point of view you may decide to take a fresh direction and you can see instantly what threads to tie up and what to do. Most people do this automatically and unconsciously. At that moment you enter a new universe of probabilities.

You may see that some attitude that you have held is not effective anymore. So you can drop it and look afresh, more consciously. A new universe of possibilities unfolds. What you want then has a greater chance of occurring. So this is a path to getting what you want.

CONCENTRATION

Unlike meditation, concentration is a focusing process. Whereas meditation is the process of emptying, concentration is a specific focusing on an internal sense to reach a desired state. For example you can use your powers of concentration to explore inner states; alter energetic patterns or habits; manifest desires and wanted experiences; and examine your daydreams or images for symbolic messages from your essence.

For example if you are feeling lethargy or apathy you may wish to focus on this feeling and allow yourself to have some mental imagery about it. Through this focusing process you in can release the blockage and attain a more energetic state. Greater understanding usually follows.

The exploration and examination of past lives is a major function of the practice of concentration. In fact hypnosis, the primary tool of past life regression, is a form of concentration. One of the best ways to study significant past lives is to focus on an area of the body which carries tension or has pain. Through concentration on the pain or tension you can begin to see, sense, or feel vivid images that often relate to past life events that continue to plague you in your present situation.

> *A medically unexplained pain in a particular area of your body could be the memory of an ancient stab wound. Your recognition releases the pain. There are often medical explanations for bodily ailments, such as arthritic pain, for which the cure can be found in past life therapy.*

Certain forms of mental imagery and guided daydreams can assist you to reach higher centers or break through to new levels of awareness. Imagery is valuable because it can be used as a metaphor to handle abstract concepts and emotions that you have had trouble naming or pinpointing. Through the use of metaphor, an exact labeling is unnecessary.

The ancient technique of the shamanic journey accompanied by drumming is a form of concentration in which you travel to inner locations of power. Here you may receive wisdom, knowledge, healing, or an infusion of personal power. Concentration in this form assists with healing emotional states as well as physical states in yourself or others.

In a similar fashion modern day psychic healing methods employ the use of visualization and concentration to channel energy and diffuse disease.

> *A good example of this is the Simontons' work with mental imagery and cancer patients. In their work, especially with children, they have achieved good healing results by instructing their patients to visualize healthy cells eating up the cancerous ones.*

There are numerous forms of concentration, also known as _yantras_ in yoga, which channel energy through your body to achieve specific states of consciousness and shifts in your energetic state.

Not everyone finds the visualization form of concentration easy to do. The visualizing process involves metaphorical muscles, so to speak, that take practice and development in order to become effective. Western society does not encourage the development of these hidden skills. Usually only those who attend art school or architectural schools obtain specific training in this area.

One form of concentration that does not necessarily involve visualization is the process of speaking inwardly to your various centers or body parts and listening for the response.

> _Imagine that you wish to ask your instinctive center to clarify what its chief concerns are. Because the instinctive center acts like the child in all of us, it responds to attention and kind responsiveness. Its concerns relate primarily to survival and basic issues. You can sit quietly and talk with your instinctive center as you would talk to a very young child._
>
> _A warrior may ask his instinctive center why he is blocked about monetary issues. The instinctive center may reply by saying that it is fearful about dying when money is the focus. It may say that in a past life he had money and was killed for it. Since these fears no longer serve him, the warrior reassures his instinctive center so it can release him to move forward._

Concentration as a form of spiritual practice primarily uses the emotional center and thus activates the expression axis.

STUDY

Study is an important spiritual tool that stimulates and develops the intellectual center. In the Far East the Hindus have called this form of spiritual exercise Raja Yoga, the approach to spirituality through intellectual discipline.

Study is the process of observing and examining events as well as your response to these events to increase understanding and expand choices.

For example some forms of modern psychotherapy facilitate this process by helping you to understand your response in a particular situation. The therapist may help you to see who you are now in the context of your own personal history. By looking at this overall context you can see your habitual responses and choose to make more appropriate choices.

Many spiritual traditions have emphasized the need for the study of spiritual texts such as the Bible or the Koran as a means of clarifying messages from master teachers. Thus each spiritual discipline recognizes the importance at least in part for study and examination.

Early Christianity is a good example of the use of study for spiritual advancement. Early Christians used to meet in people's houses to study the teachings of Christ. These meetings not only included study, but prayer and ritual. As interest grew and more people were involved the meetings in homes evolved to meetings in churches (the house of God). The function of study was formalized into the traditional sermon. The sermon then had the purpose of clarifying, in this instance, the message of Jesus Christ.

The priests, priestesses, and clergy from most religions have been highly trained and educated in order to be leaders in educating the flock.

Study may involve the reading of philosophy or sacred texts or listening to lectures and sermons, and participating in discussion. However study includes more than these activities. You study when you closely observe and examine your experience. For example Gurdjieff suggested the practice of self-photography. To practice self-photography you randomly stop whatever you are doing throughout the day and check what your thoughts and feelings are. You are then able to discover how you habitually function and eventually you develop discipline in eliminating negative thoughts and the like. This is an effective form of study.

Study is a form of spiritual practice that exercises the intellectual center and thus brings the expression axis to bear.

FASTING

Fasting is the process of eliminating food intake in order to cleanse the body and to accommodate spiritual growth. By eliminating food intake the body then begins to feed from itself and rids itself of extra fat. In this process the body purifies itself and clears out accumulated toxins.

Fasting can be quite uncomfortable at first. You may in the beginning feel ill and wish to discontinue. Headaches and body aches are common. However if you proceed through this uncomfortable state, clarity and feelings of well-being ensue. Fasting is an intricate and complex science and only a few simple words about fasting will be included here.

Severe fasting for long periods of time is extremely hard on the physical body and may even be detrimental to your health. Simple and short periodic fasting is usually best. For example eliminating food intake from one to three days, while drinking only liquids or juices, is highly effective in cleaning out toxins from the body and tuning up your ability to focus and concentrate.

There are additional cleansing processes which are described in various yoga books. However, cleansing processes should be used specifically and should not be used by everybody. In fact they should be used under the guidance of a knowledgeable physician or teacher.

Appropriate cleansing and fasting practices can open up the centers, enhance perceptivity, and bestow clarity and focus.

Fasting is strictly an instinctive center exercise and thus brings the assimilation axis to bear.

DANCE, CHANTING, MUSIC

Dancing, chanting, music, singing, and drumming are all highly energetic practices that can induce trance states to advance spiritual development. Religions and mystical groups employ one or more of these practices, usually in ritual form such as the singing of hymns in church, chanting of psalms from religious texts, and the performance of sacred dances. These are all important spiritual practices.

Visually these chants and dances have a hypnotic quality that produce the induction of a light trance. This mild trance state is a signal that the instinctive center has begun to open. As discussed earlier, through the instinctive center higher centers may be reached. With prolonged singing, chanting, or drumming the practitioner enters into the higher centers and commonly experiences ecstasy, states of high inspiration, or joy.

The use of the drum is an ancient shamanic technique which has been used in all parts of the world to facilitate trance-like states. The drum in many cultures has been called the horse or the canoe because it is like a vehicle that transports participants to other states of consciousness. The drum is effective because it cuts through intellectual and emotional center activity rapidly and allows you to enter the instinctive center state with relative ease. The higher centers are then immediately accessible.

In fact chanting and ritual dancing function according to the same principle. They produce instinctive center or trance states that clear the way to higher center activity.

There are a myriad of forms of chanting, dancing, and singing available and you must find the method and style that facilitates you the most. This of course is a matter of trial and error.

While study is a function of the intellectual center or expression axis, dancing, drumming, and singing are mostly moving centered activities and thus activate the action axis.

SERVICE

One of the ultimate goals of spirituality is the pursuit of unconditional love. Furthermore, one of the royal roads to unconditional love is service to your fellow man. Service promotes respect for others as it raises your own self-acceptance.

The majority of current cultures give only lip service to the value of service and relegate it to low-paying charity work. As a result doing service feels like you are being taken advantage of or casts you into lower class activity.

The issue of surrender looms large when you are confronted with serving others. Because your false personality looks to your individual survival, service to others at first appears like non-survival oriented activity. Surrender into giving service is in fact recognizing that you have overcome the natural inclinations of false personality and you are opening up on an essence level.

Caring for a sick friend's children, providing shelter for a homeless person or animal, and assisting an elderly relative are all traditional forms of service that may be inconvenient to false personality demands. Each requires a level of surrender so that the experience can eventually be enjoyed for its own sake.

On the other hand the ego or the false personality sometimes develops itself while masquerading as serving others.

An old saying goes, "The next best place to the top of the ladder is the bottom of the ladder." There can be much secondary gain for the person who feels victimized or enslaved while apparently serving others. When you feel victimized or martyred, you fail to take responsibility and thus eliminate personal choice and true service.

The key word here is service. When you end up feeling victimized or you feel like a doormat, you are not being selective or discriminating about the way you do formal service. True spiritual service demands self-respect and high self-esteem.

> *A good example of dignified service from the New Testament is the image of Jesus washing the feet of his apostles. It is an act deliberately chosen with a single purpose in mind. Service has been called Karma Yoga in the Hindu tradition and it is one of the highest forms of spiritual discipline.*

Finally, one of the highest forms of service is service to yourself. This includes feeding, clothing, and sheltering your body as well as making it happy by providing for it what it needs. This also includes providing all the centers with activities that feed them; intellectual input, emotional expression, and plenty of physical motion.

MEDITATIONS

Those who need meditation the most tend to resist it the most. Here is a sample meditation to help you get started. Your meditation does not have to be long, five to ten minutes to start with, and if you can work it up to fifteen or twenty minutes, you can achieve a nice balance.

The hardest thing for action roles to do in meditation is to sit there and think that you are not doing something. Do not think of meditation as doing nothing, rather think of it as actively centering yourself. You might want to include a strong visualization in the form of music or a tape that leads you through it.

Seat yourself in a neat and uncluttered environment, even a space you keep that way for the specific purpose of meditation.

Turn off your intellectual center through an act of will, a feat that will take a few moments with practice.

Say hello to all the parts of your body starting with your toes up to your head or vice versa. One minute.

Allow yourself to feel your chakras align themselves vertically and to approximately the same size. One minute.

As soon as you feel ready, ground yourself by visualizing or sensing a channel of energy falling from your instinctive center (base of spine) down to the center of the earth. Allow worries, unwanted thoughts or feelings, or any excess energy to flow out. One minute.

Allow yourself to be in touch with the energy of the universe. If it does not always work for you to put the cord down to the earth you can put the cord up and out into the universe.

Get yourself in touch with and aligned with the energy of the Tao inside you. You can begin to recognize your part in it and realize that you do not have to be in touch with it every minute to be a part of it.

Recognize that there is a plan to the universe and you can relax and flow, and things will happen and come right in the end. Take the opportunity to call upon assistance from your guides or the Tao itself. Let the Tao meditate you, after all it knows best how. Relaxation comes quickly after.

If you can experience this every single day, your body gets acclimatized to the fact that it can have the experience even when you are not meditating. However if you do not meditate on a daily basis it can be hard for you to have this occur easily.

A meditation for opening up emotional center

Deep-breathe for about five minutes. Remember that your emotional center is located in the region of your heart and lungs. If you are closed off emotionally you may be physically shut down in this area of your body. Deep breathing helps to open it up.

Stop to feel where you feel emotionally closed down. You will usually sense it in some specific part of your body. There may be pain or discomfort there or simply a feeling of numbness. It might feel like a closed-down place. Describe the sensation to yourself in terms of color, heat, shape, texture, and so on.

Visualize taking it out. Take out the withheld emotion and look at it. Examine what there is for you to know about it.

Again conceptualize its exact shape, color, and form if that is useful to you. Name it if you can.

Ask it what it is and what it has to tell you. What was it that caused you to get into that emotionally withheld state? Something triggered your habit pattern to be emotionally withheld.

You may not know at all what the trigger was, although sometimes you have a fairly good idea. Remember, however, that sometimes you are just having an emotional response that is meaningless. You think that there is a reason for it and there isn't. You are simply having an emotion. Nonetheless, take it, pull it out, and have it say what it is. It could surprise you.

Suppose, when you were three years old, you had a horrible emotional conflict with your mother while you were eating spinach. Now, every time you eat spinach you get a stomachache and you automatically withhold to some degree. That is why you don't eat spinach very often.

So you might get an insight into this process. You might say "Oh no, I am emotionally withheld every time I eat spinach? I can't believe it. I don't need to do that anymore." So you can pick up a leaf of spinach and look at it. Thank it for helping you all these years by protecting your emotional center. After all it reminded you to close it down when you perceived danger. Now your mother is not around and you don't need to close down against her getting upset. No one else is likely to be angry with you around spinach so you can let go of this protective response.

You might even feel like forgiving yourself and your mother for being angry. Your body will relax as the emotions are released. You must be willing to experience them as they let go, however.

You will find that these kinds of issues actually occur a few times a day. So you can effectively do this exercise quite often at first. As you get used to the exercise you can slip in and out of it quite readily.

Now that we have reviewed some of the basic tools for cutting through maya and accelerating spiritual growth, we are going to focus on the issue of control. What can you control? What is beyond your control? How do you surrender when you need to?

SURRENDER AND CONTROL

What aspects of your life do you have control over and what is beyond your direct control? When should you surrender to circumstances and when should you attempt to change what seems to be blocking you? These are the classic questions that arise for anyone seeking to develop spiritually. Here let us explore these questions.

Spiritually speaking, what do you control and what is beyond your control? The best way to find out for yourself is to examine your goals and desires in life. Some goals are so common that almost everyone pursues them. Here is a list of more common goals that you might want for yourself.

Love	This is the wish to unconditionally accept yourself and others. This includes friends, relatives, and perceived enemies. Love is characterized by intimacy and a feeling of connection with others.
Growth	This relates to challenges, expansion, new horizons, and the quest for enlightenment.
Fun	This is the pursuit of sensual pleasure and stimulating, satisfying experiences.
Health	This relates to a feeling of ease and balance in the body, mentally, emotionally, and spiritually.
Success	This includes money, sex, and power.
Service	This can take almost any form of action to benefit others.

Once you have focused on a goal, the next step is to work out whether or not it is within your control. If it is within your control you will find that there are ways available to achieve it.

For example if you are blinded you may be able to have an operation to repair the damage or you may be too injured to be healed. If you want to be with another you may be able to win them over to you or they may not desire it.

If there are clearly no ways available to achieve your desire then you may appropriately surrender to your position. This is not necessarily easy to determine and may take some conscious evaluation. Maya and self-deception tend to obscure the truth and an utter commitment to telling yourself the truth is often necessary to determine your course of action—whether to achieve or surrender.

Control then is a matter of degree. You can attain your desire to the extent that you are in control and your control depends on the means available to you. What then are your means?

Your means of control are as follows.

1. You are always in control of your will. Your will is capable of directing your thoughts, emotions, and actions. You have ultimate control of your responses and reactions to people, experiences, and events.

You may not be able to stop someone from taking a swing at you but you are certainly in control over your response to it. You can block and swing back, dodge and retreat, or let yourself get hit.

2. You have a certain percentage of control over situations and the universe at large.

If there is a flood you can build a boat but you may not be able to stop the torrent. If you break a leg you can speed up the healing time but you must still contend with a cast for a while.

3. You are in control of people to the extent that they give you that power.

If you are the boss you can tell people what to do but they can always quit or let you fire them. You can keep your spouse wedded to you through threats of financial abandonment but you cannot force him or her to love you.

4. Others control you to the extent that you let them.

Even if you are imprisoned, your jailers cannot control your thoughts and feelings despite the superstitions about mind control. You are always in ultimate control. If you are influenced in one way or another it is you who have allowed it.

5. On an essence level you control the events and situations of your life. Essence sets up the situations that brings you the maximum learning and evolution. If essence wishes you to recover from a painful event it will provide the means to do so. If essence has planned that you won't recover for this lifetime, so be it. When you identify with essence you are always in control. Even surrender is control.

You surrender appropriately only after you have done everything that is within your power. You can determine if you have done so by knowing and telling the truth. That is, you become aware of what essence wants.

The Seven Steps to Surrender

What do you do when an obstacle arises that is clearly beyond your control? The process of coming to terms with that obstacle can be viewed as having seven steps.

1. You notice the obstacle.

Examples: Your mate wants to leave you.
           You contract a serious disease.
           You are sued and face bankruptcy.
           You lose a limb in an accident.
           You are given notice at work.
           Your application for school has been rejected.
           You are burglarized.
           A close friend dies suddenly.

2. You ignore it. You deny it. It can't be happening and you hope if you just don't think about it, it will go away.

Examples: You go on making plans as if nothing were wrong.
           You fantasize a lot about the way things were.
           You smile, put on a brave front and tell everyone
               you are fine.

3. It won't go away so you resist it and fight it. This becomes a major struggle.

Examples: You take drugs or drink to avoid the pain.
           You try to do all the things you used to do when
               things were like they were.

4. You react with anger and frustration. The struggle has continued beyond what feels fair and reasonable. You feel a victim of the situation.

Examples: You blame others for the situation.
           You want revenge and retribution.
           You attack even those close to you.
           You wail and cry in grief.

5. You plea bargain and appeal to the highest authority. You agree to anything. You sell your soul in desperation. You try the most extreme and unlikely options.

> Examples: You start praying and go to church.
> You try strange remedies that make you more ill.
> You try a crash diet or promise to give up your vices.
> You donate vast sums of money to charity.
> You agree to put up with your mate having other lovers at home.

6. You are resigned. You have tried everything to no avail. You give up in hopelessness. You could stay in despair for a long time.

> Examples: You sink into deep depression.
> You withdraw from everyone.
> You drink yourself into the ground.
> You become careless about your safety and act recklessly.
> You become disheveled, apathetic, and listless.

7. You surrender. You experience peace and tranquility. You feel complete and you do not feel bad anymore. You accept what is and you feel rather indifferent to your former struggle. You ultimately receive a treasure that you had wished for all along. It may not be what you thought you wanted in the struggle. It is a gift that is better.

> Examples: You discover a hidden talent.
> You have major insights and breakthroughs in your understanding of yourself.
> You experience profound relaxation and resulting joy.

You make new friends, move to a better location,
or find a better job.
You discover love for yourself.

Life is set up so that this process does not come easily and much is learned through the experience. Children under five and adults over fifty-five are often able to surrender more than those in between. By being able to surrender more easily they have more control and are consequently more powerful.

Remember that ultimate control rests with identifying with essence. Even surrender then becomes control.

RESPONSIBILITY

What are you directly responsible for in your life and what is not your responsibility but rather the responsibility of others? This is another critical question that arises on the path of spiritual evolution. To be able to answer this question you must know what responsibility truly is.

To be responsible is to respond appropriately and exercise control whether it be surrender or perseverance toward your goal. Ultimately responsibility is your ability to act moment-to-moment from your innermost integrity. This means that no matter what guidance you receive from teachers, spiritual systems, or friends, you ultimately make the choices and reap the consequences of those choices.

Responsibility is not duty nor is it actions based on shoulds and oughts. These by definition are limiting and carry with them the seeds of martyrdom, the antithesis of responsibility.

The question of responsibility arises immediately when you attempt to go after what you want. You spend your life in hot pursuit of whatever you deem important. Along the way you are constantly thwarted and sidetracked. As a result you can easily fall prey to several pitfalls. Firstly, you may feel that you are

are a victim and can never get what you want and you may feel that someone else is responsible for the fortunes in your life.

> *For example you may blame others for your perceived misfortunes such as losing your job or your relationship. When fortuitous events occur you can chalk it up to chance, coincidence, or the benevolence of a whimsical god.*

Secondly you may take the opposite point of view and grandiosely feel that you are responsible for everything and everyone's experience, good and bad as you judge it.

> *If a plane crashes with the loss of everyone on board you may erroneously believe that your negative thoughts caused the deaths of many innocent people. This leads to terrible guilt and self-judgment. Indeed children of age two frequently make this error. On the other hand you may mistakenly believe that you are so powerful that you are keeping all the other planes in the sky from crashing. Again this is a narcissistic point of view that does not jibe with reality.*

Victimization and martyrdom are blocks to taking responsibility. Likewise, seeing your false personality as all-powerful and responsible for everything is a block to true responsibility. This is nothing more than grandiosity, a super maya, covering up intense insecurity and feelings of victimization.

Responsibility has more to do with you stating what you want and then being willing to have it. Why do you resist this simple truth? There are some common reasons that arise from the illusion of your false personality.

1. Getting what you want makes you wrong about not being able to have it. Nobody likes to be wrong. You often would rather be right and not have than wrong and have.

2. Getting what you want eliminates excuses and complaining. These are addictions of the false personality, tough to break.

3. Getting what you want feels impossible because you feel too inadequate to get it or have it (self-deprecation).

4. Getting what you want instills in you the fear that you may be selfish and depriving someone else of what they want (poverty consciousness).

5. Getting what you want might cause you to have to take responsibility in all parts of your life and this feels too hard.

6. Getting what you want is terrifying because you might enjoy it immensely and then lose it only to feel horrible grief and loss.

7. Getting what you want may feel so good that you don't feel you can handle the energy or pleasure of the experience. It might make you feel so uncomfortable that you feel like you are dying.

8. Getting what you want spells the end of the game, introducing the unknown future which is terrifying.

In the next chapter we will focus on getting help from outside the physical plane. First we will discuss the help that spirit guides afford you and then we will discuss how to channel for greater conscious assistance.

Chapter Four

Guides and Channeling

SPIRIT GUIDES

Each person on the physical plane has friends and helpers who are not occupying a physical body but have their being on one of the higher planes. These friends and helpers, whom we may call spirit guides, are often members of your own entity who are between lifetimes. In many cases the principal spirit guide is your essence twin, if your essence twin is in fact between lives.

Since spirit guides exist outside the physical plane, they are outside its limitations of time and space as well. They have access to information about the past, about the future and about events that may be taking place far away.

These friends and helpers offer assistance in a variety of ways. They can act as teachers, healers, and providers of knowledge both for yourself or for other people through you. You may have one recognized spirit guide or literally hundreds. Sometimes you work with only one, or perhaps with a variety, each specializing in a different area.

> For example, you could call on a spirit guide who is adept at finding lost objects or another who helps you to relax and heal yourself. You can consult still another who is knowledgeable about the psychological dynamics of your relationships.

Although everyone has helpers such as these, many people are not aware of them consciously. Younger souls are usually unaware of them whereas older souls begin to become more conscious of them. Older souls start to recognize them, call upon them consciously and actively employ them. The extent to which this happens depends enormously upon the culture and prevailing belief system that surrounds the old soul.

You can make conscious contact with your spirit guides through meditation and visualization. Your spirit guides communicate with you in a number of ways. They usually communicate through the chakra system, the subtle or energetic organs of the body.

If you communicate with your guide through the fifth chakra, you will hear the guide mentally. Perhaps you will allow your throat and voice to vocalize the communication of your guide. This is known as channeling.

Sixth chakra communication will be characterized by mental pictures shown to you by your guide. You may have to interpret these symbols or images or ask the guide for further clarification.

If you do some kind of healing work including nursing, doctoring, massage, dentistry, acupuncture, or bodywork, the spirit guide may establish contact through your hands. Your hands will be guided to the problem area on the client's body and healing energy will then be channeled through you from the guide.

You may visualize your spirit guide as male or female, or you may identify them by a particular name and may see them dressed in a manner consistent with a past culture. These are common ways of symbolizing spirit guides, as they appeared once in a particular lifetime. Perhaps this is how you remember them best from a past lifetime when you knew them.

A guide might appear to you as a native American, a Chinese acupuncturist, an African witch doctor, a Tibetan lama, a rabbi or what have you.

Spirit guides make themselves available to care for their friends who are in physical bodies and endeavoring to cope with the physical plane. They may also be creating or repaying karma of a helpful kind.

Sometimes they are entities who have cycled off the physical plane but still wish to offer assistance. The most powerful healers are those who acknowledge assistance from what they would call a higher power or their spirit guides.

Occasionally a person who is having difficulty with his own sense of identity and his own boundaries may not be able to identify the spirit guides as non-physical and may see them as real people. This may then be classified as hallucinating or as a psychotic episode. In fact the person is simply having difficulty distinguishing between the astral plane and the physical plane. They are confused about time and space and are uncertain about what is actually real. This does not mean however that their experience is to be entirely dismissed nor does it mean that they are incapable of healing.

In working with spirit guides it is helpful to request their help consciously and to direct their activities, or refuse their help as the case may be. Although spirit guides are unhampered by time and space and have a great store of helpful information at hand, they are not in a physical body like you, and therefore not in the most powerful position to heal. You, the healer in the body, are always senior to the spirit guide.

The following is an exercise to help you make contact with a spirit guide.

> Sit in a relaxed position with eyes closed; take several deep breaths and make the silent request to communicate with and identify the spirit guides. Ask that only the one or few that are appropriate for you today to come forward.

> Begin to visualize on the outside of your aura (around your body from about eighteen inches to two feet outwards) a figure, usually that of a person, although it can be an animal. Ask the spirit guide to give a name and to identify him or herself. Look to see how the individual is dressed, or if you cannot picture them, notice what their energy feels like.

> You may ask the spirit guide silently what kind of assistance they are capable of giving.

> When you have finished communicating it is appropriate to thank the spirit guide and ask that the spirit guide be available whenever you have the need for their services either for yourself or others. Remember that they want to help regardless of what you feel your own worthiness is.

The more one communicates with spirit guides the more available they are for help.

CHANNELING

Michael on Channeling

What is channeling? Channeling is simply the ability to act as a vehicle for the communication and teaching of an essence that is not your own. For example, this teaching is a channeled teaching. We are the non-physical teacher and there are a variety of people who act as channels for us. So, what is involved in channeling? Can only certain people do it? How do they? Is it hard or easy? What does it feel like? Well, here you will find the answers to these questions and more.

Why channel? Experienced entities who have graduated and cycled off from the physical plane often wish to offer their assistance and help to those still living on the planet. On the physical plane communication depends on having a physical body with vocal cords that can speak or hands that can write. Since cycled-off beings no longer have bodies to communicate with, they have to briefly borrow a body or part of one to get their message across. This must be done only with the absolute agreement of the person whose body is to be used for the communication. This person is called a channel or medium.

In order to become good at channeling, the channel must learn several manipulations. First he must learn to relax and get his own essence out of the way as much as possible so as to allow the fullest possible expression of the being wishing to communicate. This means surrendering control of what is said, what is written, or what is done with the hands. This takes practice and with time the channel becomes clearer and clearer, communicating with a minimum amount of distortion.

When a channel is inexperienced or just starting out, the message of the entity is often filtered through the personality of the channel. This means that at times there can be a fair amount of distortion in the channeling. If the channel has some strong beliefs in a particular area, these beliefs can color or distort the quality of the information coming through.

> *For example, if the channel was once raped by a man, it may be difficult for her to neutrally and clearly channel information about male sexuality. She would first have to come to terms with this experience and practice letting go in order to successfully channel this subject matter.*

CHANNELING

The accuracy of the channeling is dependent on a great many factors. Illness, fatigue, and the nature of the questions or the information can all serve to distort the clarity of the channeling. Even when a channel is experienced and exceptionally good there may be some distortion of the information. On a good day the channeling may be eighty-five percent correct. On a poor day the accuracy of the information may drop to only fifty percent. For this reason we caution you never to believe what a channel says but to check out the information for yourself first. Does it feel accurate? Does it fit with other things you know or have learned? Can it be verified by your own experience? These are some of the questions to ask yourself about any channeled information.

Who can Channel

Most people have the ability to channel, however some have a natural talent for it. Of course many people who are capable of channeling either have no desire to do so or do not realize that they can. Soul level and role have little to do with channeling ability. However the soul level of the channel will certainly effect the level of information that is communicated.

> *An infant soul medium might channel information that has a superstitious flavor while a baby soul channel's rendering of the message may be in terms of hellfire and brimstone and so on. A young soul's presentation of the message will likely direct power and attention toward the channel himself. Older souls will tend to channel simpler messages that have a universal application.*

Not all channels are alike. Some people are more adept at channeling specific information about particular subject matters. Since the entity who wishes to speak must use the channel's vocabulary, the channel's acquaintance with a subject matter makes a big difference. A channel with a knowledge of internal medicine would be able to communicate much better about forms of healing than a channel without this knowledge. A channel with a working knowledge of physics would be more adept channeling these abstract concepts than another without the vocabulary. Channels with a knowledge of history are often best at pinpointing past lives and elucidating the events of past eras.

Informational channels do not all use the same methods. Some go into a partial trance and with pen in hand do automatic writing. They do not have conscious control of the flow of words onto the paper but they simply read with surprise what they are writing. This can be accomplished on a typewriter as well. A few use a Ouija board to spell out the letters to form words and messages. Most channels eventually move on to verbal channeling because of its rapidity and ease. Some close their eyes while some leave them open. Some take on a distinct and unique way of speaking and some retain their own speaking style. Some are dramatic and some quite dry. The important thing to remember is that there is no right way and no wrong way. What is essential is the quality of the message.

Some channels are not good at transmitting information at all but are much better at channeling art, music, and songs. Others, especially priests, are best at channeling pure healing energy with no informational content at all. They simply lay their hands on the patient and channel healing energy, directing it to the malady or area of disease.

How to channel

Now, since you have a physical body and that physical body is occupied by your essence, we could say that you always channel your own essence into your body. That's how natural and easy it can be. Channeling a different essence into your body can take some getting used to. First of all you may experience a different sensation in your body. Your body may feel much more solid than it usually does, or it may feel much more fluid than usual.

In order to channel you will have to be as clear and balanced as possible. You are raising and increasing the amount of energy you are used to having in your body and this can have a variety of effects. If you are not balanced you can end up with a severe headache, neckache, buzzing sensation, nausea, muscle twitches, or sleeplessness.

Also, when you start increasing the amount of energy in your body this can activate your instinctive center, causing you to be flooded with anxiety or fears. There is no harm in this as long as you are prepared to work through any of your unresolved issues as you go along. It is best to have some support for this. If you ever feel overwhelmed it is best to back off for a while and channel for very brief periods of time.

Here are a few pointers to get you started channeling if this is your wish.

1. Sit comfortably with your spine straight, preferably not after a heavy meal. Although you can channel anywhere, at first it is best to have a safe comfortable spot where you can get into the mood easily.

2. Align and balance your chakras using your powers of imagination or visualization. Your chakras should be vertically in a line, each about the same size and open from front to back. This need take only a moment after you have practiced.

3. Imagine a golden lace cloak that you can toss over yourself for protection against interference from others' thoughts and communications that might be distracting to you. Leave a small opening at the crown.

4. Request the entity of your choice. Ask for Michael, one of your own spirit guides, or any other entity that you would like to channel. Postulate that your cooperation will be of mutual benefit and that you will feel great upon finishing.

5. Imagine the entity flowing down through the crown of your head, into your body, and down your spinal column through your chakras. In general the lower you can bring the energy of the entity into your body the better channeling you will be able to do. Feel it all the way down to the base of your spine.

6. Experience whatever subjective feelings and sensations occur to you.

7. Begin to speak whatever thoughts come into your head without censorship. Do not be concerned if they feel like your own or not. The entity's communication through you and with you is often undramatic and may not feel unusual. Trust that what you say is the entity's communication. After a while you will get used to certain cues that let you know you are channeling.

Here are some possible cues!

1. You feel a surge of power through your body.

2. You feel tingling up your spine or at the crown of your head.

3. You feel surprised at how effortlessly words and phrases come out of your mouth.

4. You say things you didn't know you knew.

5. You feel absolute certainty when you speak.

6. Your mouth feels funny.

7. The energy in your body feels different, either more solid or more fluid.

8   You feel stuck to your seat.

9. You have a solid or strange feeling at the pit of your stomach.

10. Your vision seems different somehow. Colors look different, perhaps brighter.

You have seen how this teaching fits into the larger context of spiritual growth. You have learned the importance of being awake and aware on the spiritual path and the value of balance in that process. You have become acquainted with the obstacles on the spiritual path in the form of maya and you have gained some understanding of control and surrender as a way through the illusion. Finally you have reviewed the major methods and techniques to further your awareness and cut through the hypnosis of the physical plane.

In the next part we will focus in greater depth on the various kingdoms you associate with on the Earth. You will then see how these kingdoms interact with your personality and you will discover how they affect your overleaves. Finally, you will be exposed to some of the major planetary tools available for spiritual guidance and growth.

PART TWO

RELATING TO THE PLANET

Chapter Five

The Power of Nature

Part II: Integration

In part II we will review your progression through the seven earthly kingdoms and elaborate on how each builds upon the last to prepare you for human form. We will explore the world of devas in greater detail and help you to understand how you can communicate with them and gain assistance from them, resulting in mutual benefit.

Here we will also focus on the primary tools of the planet and show you how to use them appropriately and productively for spiritual guidance and advancement.

DEVAS

You have seen how you sprang from the Tao as sparks of light to become fragments of an entity or family of consciousness. As a fragment you have taken multiple human lives, progressing in the difficult fast-learning school of earth through the infant to old soul stages in order to contribute to your entity's overall experience.

Now let us return to the time before you became human. Remember that you did not arrive on the planet in the first lifetime of the infant soul stage directly from the Tao. Who and what were you before you took the human form? How did you prepare for your first human lives? In this section you will learn in more detail how you chose to leave the womb of the Tao to develop your relationship with the physical plane. Here we will review the progressive steps from birth as a fragment to your first infant soul lifetime.

Not surprisingly, inorganic and organic matter on Earth is divided into seven kingdoms of ascending order of diversity and complexity. As primordial units of consciousness and energy you begin to live through each of these kingdoms according to a specific order. These seven concentrations of experience are as follows:

KINGDOM	ALSO INCLUDES:
1. OCEANIC/MINERAL	All grand scale experience: ocean, wind, clouds. Mountain, minerals; gems.
2. PLANT/VEGETABLE	Plants: herbs, spices
3. INSECTS	Bacteria, microbes worms; bugs, spiders, crustaceans.
4. FISH, REPTILES	
5. BIRDS	
6. LOWER MAMMALS & BIRDS OF PREY	Mice, sheep, goats, cows, antelope, eagles, hawks, parrots, and more.
7. HIGHER MAMMALS	Gorillas, canines, felines, boar, bear, horses, and others of high intelligence.

Each kingdom represents a grand spectrum of experience and a great range of complexity. In the first three kingdoms you experience life as Devas, beings who protect, tend, and experience the life of rock formations, weather patterns, and plant life. These Devas have been acknowledged and referred to throughout history as sprites, spirits, and leprechauns.

Shakespeare's play A Midsummer Night's Dream _portrays his concept of the activities of these earth spirits and how they can interact with the world of men. According to Shakespeare, the Devas are playful and mischievous, creatively interfering with the couples who wander into the woods on a midsummer's night. This is not far from the truth because Devas are experimenters who, although they may appear to humans as tricksters, are really going about their business in a playful, creative way._

Devas experiment and play with the primary forces of nature, molding and combining them in ever new ways to create new forms, new species, new genetic experiences. After millions upon millions of years of Devic activity, earth has been prepared for sentient life. Devas actively prepare and mold species toward eventually becoming ensouled. A species must have developed the intellectual center in order to be ready for infant soul status.

The work of Devas today is oriented more towards protecting and preserving life forms than the earlier enormously creative challenge of preparing the environment from organic soup to its present form. Still Devas help to prepare more species in their development of the intellectual center. Currently gorillas are the most advanced of all mammals besides cetaceans and humans and a very few of these are approaching first level infant soul status.

Devas prefer to experience and inhabit natural forms that they can contribute to in some fashion. Man-made objects are of less interest because they have already been formed and the creative process is complete.

DEVAS

Since Devas are incorporeal, they do not experience time as humans do. For them, occupying a Redwood tree for several thousand years is interesting and may be experienced as no more than the blink of an eye. Since Devas are infinitely compressible or expandable, hundreds of them may occupy a single flower, or one may inhabit an entire cloud formation.

The life of Devas is organized according to the greater plan set up by the Tao. Within these infinitely detailed plans is great room for on-the-spot creativity. One might say the Devas are the fingers of the Tao.

Let us now examine each of the developmental kingdoms and discover the role of the Devas within them. Remember that these devas are more primitive versions of you. They are part of you and what you have experienced.

OCEANIC/MINERAL KINGDOM

The oceanic or mineral kingdom is the most basic and least diversified experience available on the physical plane and more specifically on earth. Here, as part of your entire cadre in Devic form, you experience and give consciousness to whole mountain ranges for periods of up to thousands of years. Whole land masses are experienced on different parts of the globe in order to feel and know the variety of geological formations such as plates, strata, and rock formations extant on the planet. You experience varieties of transformations at this level such as earthquakes, volcanic activity, stresses, tensions, erosion, upheavals and the like. Whether these massive experiences are enjoyable or not is unimportant because you seek after all variety of experience.

As Devas you help to form these massive formations and experiment with the possibilities inherent in them. Each experiment leads the planet closer to supporting more complex life forms.

In addition to land mass activity you meld with such large-scale phenomena as oceans, winds, clouds, rivers, and lakes. For example, after several thousand years as a sea, experiencing shore-to-shore tidal movements, currents, temperature gradients, and a myriad of life forms within, a cadre will relinquish the habitat to another cadre desiring this experience. Often, when such a shift occurs, the nature of the sea or land mass will change as the new awareness seeks to experiment with its physical form. This may mark the beginning of intensive earthquakes or dramatic volcanic activity. Because all consciousness at this level is still closely identified with the Tao, all of these experiments and creative maneuvers are in harmony with a master plan for the planet.

As humans, you may experience a certain affinity for geographical locations that you once experienced in a much less diversified form. For example, you may have experienced a portion of land mass that now makes up a part of the Grand Canyon, a place you love to visit.

These locations may be a source of power or inspiration for the person who knows the area intimately from pre-sentient awareness.

This accounts for the age-old shamanic belief in personal places of power as well as the belief that spirits are in rocks, mountains, and all physical locations. In fact infant souls, being closer to the Tao, often recognize the consciousness in inorganic material; however they often fear it. This awareness is usually forgotten until the older soul ages, when the aliveness of all things is once again remembered without fear.

The exalted role of priest and the ordinal role of server tend to enjoy the oceanic aspect of this kingdom the most. These roles tend to be inspired by displays of weather such as sunsets, cloud formations, and the sea.

On the other hand the action roles of warrior and king enjoy the experience of Devas who specialize in more solid formations such as mountain ranges and rock formations. These roles have a special affinity for mountains such as John Muir's [king] special devotion to the Sierras.

When a Deva is satisfied with its experience of overwhelming physical phenomena, it is ready to move on to more focused awareness of a mineral nature.

This more specialized experience includes more specific, complex compounds such as crystals, gemstones, and all the various metals. At this level, consciousness in the form of Devas specializes in more local experiences where it can learn the exact nature of its effects on the surrounding forms. Metals and gems have a direct effect on the environment and more interestingly can be used by humans as tools for particular ends. In this way the consciousness in these compounds begins to learn about sentience by being in direct relationship to it. In a way, it could be said that gems and minerals taught man how to use them so they could evolve.

Metals could be extricated from the earth, refined, and put into pragmatic or artistic form. These metals could then play a direct part in the events of men. In fact history is full of references to objects made of metals such as gold, silver, and lead, that have a beneficial or negative effect on people.

In a similar fashion, gemstones have played a significant part in the development of technology and art. The diamond for example is highly regarded for its beauty as well as its utility as a superstrong cutter. Crystals are valued for beauty, for occult purposes, and for their function in electronic technology.

Why do certain gems have such a powerful appeal to many people while other gemstones seem to repel them? It is simply that gems have consciousness and are aware physical forms. They are alive and experience a level of greater uniqueness and diversity than in their prior habitats.

Gems and crystal forms vibrate at specific frequencies that result in pronounced effects on other forms of life. Animals and men are attracted to areas where certain gems abound in the earth and will avoid areas where other gems cluster.

Historically the effects of certain gems became known to some people who used them as tools and talismans, wearing them to alter their moods, enhance their dreams, or affect their personalities. Kings, queens, and popes wore crowns and carried scepters heavily encrusted with valuable gems not only to demonstrate wealth but to become empowered and gain control.

Indigenous peoples wear local gems expressively and decoratively as well as for beneficial effects on health and mood.

> *The Navajo Indians of Arizona, for example, wear an abundance of turquoise to elevate their expressive sensibilities and achieve the higher emotional center. The Navajos like many Native American peoples know that metals and rocks are alive and are to be revered as sacred forms of the Great Spirit or the Tao.*

Within this teaching specific gemstones enhance or retard the effects of all of the personality overleaves. A basic list of these gemstones and their interrelationships is included in the next section.

The action roles of king and warrior favored the Devic experiences related to metals and crystal formation. These more solid materials are in affinity with the solidity of the action roles. Many warriors and kings enjoy working with minerals and metals because of their special affinity for them. King Solomon's mines are a case in point or you might imagine King Arthur with his famous inscribed sword, Excalibur.

Upon completion of the experience of gemstones and metals, Devas may choose to move toward sentience by entering the plant/vegetable kingdom.

PLANT/VEGETABLE KINGDOM

The vegetable kingdom includes all plant life from the most nonspecific to the most unique. In the earlier forms of this experience, consciousness may choose to become an entire meadow with its accompanying grasses and mosses whose roots intertwine and whose existence depends entirely upon millions of its own kind in close proximity. Gradually the being moves into more unique, more individualized forms of plantlife, often experimenting with mutations and entirely new forms within a particular species. Trees such as Oaks, Elms, Maples, and Redwoods represent the more individualized, more separate forms of plantlife. At this level of development consciousness experiences several kinds of environments at once. The tree's roots live under the surface of the earth while its trunk may rise to great heights to experience the atmosphere there.

Plants then learn to act as natural bridges and translators between highly different natural environments.

Like gems and metals, plants creatively interact with other lifeforms. By their very nature plants are even more capable of affecting and being affected by all the various kingdoms; stone, mineral, insect, fish, bird, and mammal. Plants depend upon weather to survive. They rely on minerals and metals to provide essential ingredients for development and propagation. Insects and worms facilitate or retard their growth and often are relied on for reproduction. Fish, reptiles, and birds feed upon them and live among them, further enhancing their experience of being and encouraging their developmental process. Likewise mammals and humans live among plant life, depending upon them for their very sustenance.

Plants have a special relationship with humans in that they allow men to cultivate them and creatively reproduce them for medicinal purposes, fuel, shelter, food, and a wide variety of products. This relationship between plant and human then is highly beneficial to both because each enjoys and learns much from the other. Plants are capable of great intimacy with man because they are actually consumed by them and become part of their flesh. This allows plant consciousness to experience being a part of a human body that is occupied by sentient consciousness. In this way plants approximate human life long before taking on the complexity of becoming an infant soul.

As with clouds, mountains, and gems, plants have their own kind of power and truly are inspirited as the shamans of old have always known. Because of a past experience living as a variety of plant, you may have a special relationship with that plant. You may have a green thumb for its cultivation or a special talent in understanding its helpful properties and gifts. For example a carpenter may experience a special affinity for redwood or rosewood because of a previous association with it. He may be able to work wonders with it while other equally skilled carpenters avoid it or lack interest in it.

You may regard a particular plant as a special ally and use that plant to heal yourself or others. You know the language of that plant so to speak because at some level you are able to tune into the spiritual life there.

The expressive role of sage loves the experience of those Devas who specialize in the plant/vegetable kingdom because of the tremendous expressive qualities of plantlife. Think of Carmen Miranda [artisan] with a huge bowl of fruit on her head.

When spirit feels complete with the plant/vegetable kingdom the choice is made whether to proceed to insect life.

INSECTS

Life begins in the insect kingdom in simple bodies that rely on bigger hosts for survival. Gradually these simple forms of insect life give way to more and more separate and individual types.

As insects, consciousness begins to experience more mobility than its prior plantlife experience. Migration, colonization, and predation become much more rapid. Complex interrelationships are developed within and between species. Many insects such as termites, ants, and bees establish structured colonies, highly complex societies in which specialties are developed and used for the benefit of the whole colony. For example soldier ants protect the colony from attack by other insects while worker ants forage for food and build the nest for the shelter of the entire colony. An exalted queen ant is protected and defended for her ability to lay all the eggs needed by the colony for propagation. Specialized ants care for her eggs while others may carefully tend and milk a slave colony of aphids kept for their nourishing juices.

Insect life, then, offers the possibility of independent mobility in a specialized body that can live under the ground, on land, in the water, or in the air. Through insect life, consciousness becomes able to greatly expand its experience of the entire planet. Like plants, insects can live inside other living organisms and thus experience the life there from an integral vantage point. Parasites live out their entire lives on the backs of, or inside of fish, birds, and mammals. Again, insects are able to interact with man from this unique perspective.

Other larger insects are able to establish a relationship with humans, sometimes even being kept as pets or playmates. Many a prisoner has enjoyed the company of a beetle or spider who shared his lonely cell.

The expressive role of artisan particularly enjoys the insect kingdom because of its fluidity and rapid pace. Insects mutate rapidly giving rise to tremendous creative and expressive potential. This, then, naturally leads toward what the role of artisan likes to do the most: rapidly create.

Artisans often draw creative ideas from observing the colors and forms of the insect world.

When consciousness feels complete with insect life it then may choose to experiment with fish and reptile life.

FISH AND REPTILES

The kingdom of fish and reptiles offers a more massive experience in a unique mobile body than any prior lifeform. Life as a tuna or boa constrictor offers the possibility of a more stable existence than that of a moth for example. These lifeforms have a more individualized personality than the insects and develop a character of their own. Many experience a kind of primitive family life as they gather for protection and feeding.

Although each fish and reptile has its own personality no matter how slight, it actually belongs to a hive soul that has many members. Each fish or reptile then is like a cell in this hive soul's body. The loss of one or several cells does not hurt the main body and often actually helps it to stay healthy.

For this reason, fish and reptiles allow individuals to be preyed on by other species and by one another. Reptiles and fish have long had this kind of relationship with man, even letting men know in intuitive ways where schools could be found for hunting purposes. Of course this relationship has been based on a special balance, not distorted by greed or destruction. Today's fishing techniques violate this natural balance, causing whole species to become extinct. The destruction of the great sea turtle is a case in point. Too many cells have been taken and the hive souls of the sea turtle may have to withdraw from physical form. This deprives consciousness of one of the wonderful choices it has had to play upon the earth.

Throughout history people have revered fish and reptiles, sometimes honoring them as gods. They knew that these life forms were aware and that they not only symbolized life but they were consciousness itself. They knew that the fish, reptile, and human source of life was the Tao.

When fish and reptile (and amphibian) life has been experienced to full satisfaction, consciousness makes the choice whether or not to go on to the bird kingdom.

BIRDS

Much that has been said about fish and reptiles applies to birds as well. Their bodies offer even greater mobility and they have developed a significant tool for independence. Their bodies are warm-blooded, freeing them from total dependence on conditions of climate and permitting them to move about freely. Whereas a cold-blooded lizard becomes dormant when the temperature drops, many species of birds can tolerate a great range of temperatures and climates, from snow and ice to desert and jungle.

Like fish and reptiles, most birds have hive souls that include an entire flock. Not all members of the flock need be together however in order to survive, as is the case with captive birds and more solitary birds like egrets and hummingbirds.

Many birds live in colonies and experience a complex social life that includes a pecking order, male and female courtship ritual, migration, and mutual cooperation in rearing young. In fact birds begin to experience prolonged family life in that fledglings require a longer period of care and nurturance than do reptiles and fish. Birds are not born with an immediate ability to survive like the fish and reptile kingdom. They have foregone some instinct for the sake of different kinds of family life.

Whereas, personality-wise, one type of fish is much like another, birds have developed unique personalities even among the same species.

As with prior life forms, consciousness specializes in a great variety of experiences through the bird kingdom. Some are scavengers like the vultures that roam the landscape on thermals in search of carrion, contributing to the mass cleanup efforts of nature. Others are ice specialists like the penguin while others like the seagull prefer the sea as their environment.

The assimilation role of scholar specializes in the bird kingdom and in fact were responsible for the development of birds as a variety of species. Because of this, scholars may often be found working with birds, bird-watching, and studying their habits and habitats.

Birds and Roles:

Priest:	Flamingo
Server:	Pigeon
Sage:	Parakeet, Tanager, Oriole
Artisan:	Nightingale
King:	Canary
Warrior:	Woodpecker, Hummingbird
Scholar:	Hawk, Falcon, Parrot, Cockatoo

(Note: Some of these belong to the kingdom of lower mammals and birds of prey discussed next.)

When Bird awareness feels complete, consciousness may choose to continue on to the kingdom of lower mammals and birds of prey.

KINGDOM OF LOWER MAMMALS/BIRDS OF PREY

Lower mammals and birds of prey, like most animals, have hive souls that often herd together for mutual cooperation, protection, family, and friendship. Mammals even more than birds offer the potential of a lengthy child-rearing experience where the intimacies of family life as well as tribal life may be savored. During this long-term childhood, emotions and behaviors are learned and practiced. Once again instincts have been reduced in favor of more individualized and creative personal expression.

In addition to warm-bloodedness, mammals have the further advantage of experiencing live birth, a profound, intense, emotion-filled event that impacts all of life. This sets the stage for the experience of birth as a human being or cetacean.

Mammals and birds of prey, more than any other prior kingdom, have the option to work in harmony with men. While many animals experience lives totally in the wild, some actively seek out the company of men in order to interact creatively with them. Over centuries certain types of animals have given up their unique independent lives in the wild in order to become the slaves of men and serve them through the use of their products and talents in exchange for care and protection.

Although one could argue that these poor creatures were taken advantage of by men who robbed them of their independence and harnessed them for work and meat, this is not the case. For to say that,is to consider mammals as victims with no choices of their own. Certain species of mammals and birds made the choice to submit to men in order to do creative projects with them. Although this agreement has been badly abused at times, there has been overall benefit to man and mammal.

Like reptiles and birds, different species of mammals represent creative specialties, designed to gain a specific perspective of life on earth. Certainly giraffe-ness is different from mouse-ness, and Seal lives a totally different life from Deer. As consciousness begins to favor one or other mammal experience, you can see the specialties that lead to certain essence roles in human form. Warriors tend to enjoy bear lives, for example; sages favor otter lives; and the servers of the world prefer the experience of the elephant lifetimes. Scholars enjoy the hawk experience the most because they are similar in terms of vision and assimilation. Sages are more often parakeet specialists, while priests favor the inspirational expression of the llama. Scholars are those devas who enjoy the mammal experience the most and they are the role that remembers their animal heritage the most.

HIGHER MAMMALS

The kingdom of higher mammals, seventh of the evolutionary series, represents the most complex, individual, and unique experience available before becoming an infant soul human being or cetacean. These are the animals that tend to have the most individual experience of themselves and manifest the most unique personalities of all the animals. They can be tool users and demonstrate an extraordinary level of intelligence. Some are capable of rudimentary symbol usage and communicate with humans at an advanced level.

The higher mammals include river dolphins, higher primates, felines large and small, canines, horses, boars, grizzly bears, and other animals known for their extraordinary intelligence. Some of them spend their entire lives in the company of humans, learning from them and preparing themselves for the first infant soul life.

As with the prior kingdom, one deva usually accompanies the life of one individual animal and not the whole herd, flock, or school. Each animal has a life of its own and the deva only associates with and experiences the animal's life in company with it for one lifetime.

Mammals and Roles

Priest	Zebra, Llama
Server	Elephant
Sage	Otter, Orangutan, Muskrat
Artisan	Deer, Platypus
King	Bull
Warrior	Bear, Gorilla
Scholar	All animals

KINGDOMS AND ROLES

Kingdom	Role
Oceanic/mineral, Clouds,sea, weather	Priest, Server
Mountain; metals, minerals, gems	Warrior, King
Plant/vegetable	Sage
Insect	Artisan
Reptiles and Fish	All roles
Bird	Scholar
Lower Mammals	Scholar
Birds of prey	Scholar
Higher mammals	All roles

ANIMAL LIFETIMES

The animal itself has a reincarnational series of seven lifetimes in one species. So, for example, a cat or dog has seven lives in a series. Each animal remembers all prior lifetimes completely and will often manifest fears and preferences that it adopted in former lives. This helps to give the more advanced animals their special personalities.

An animal that has a special relationship to a human will often attempt to return to the association with that human in the successive life because it has had a good experience with them. Pets often do this.

DEVAS AND HUMAN BEINGS

Devas exist outside of time and do not experience death as do the physical forms they accompany. Although each of you fully evolved through the seven kingdoms in devic form, even now you are connected with the ongoing existences of all your devic lives. For human beings, the focus of consciousness is in the current lifetime and not in your myriad simultaneous devic lives. Often you can subconsciously tap into these devic parts of yourself and make use of their knowledge of this or that kingdom. As mentioned earlier, you may manifest certain talents such as a green thumb or uncanny ability to forecast the weather. You can, however, consciously dip into your devic selves and become a powerful shaman, healer, mystic, scientist, or inventor. You can discover that power is sourced in evolutionary progress into what appears to be past as well as evolutionary progress toward the future.

Scholars and priests represent opposite sides of this spectrum. While priests forge ahead and propel mankind into visions of the future, scholars keep track of the whole of what has been, and try to remind mankind not to forget the power of lessons learned.

TOOLS OF THE PLANET

In addition to having a body of flesh and blood, being on the physical plane means learning to understand and use the physical environment appropriately. Everything in your environment—water, oil, rocks, metals, plants, animals, and their derivatives—have both physical properties and spiritual properties and ultimately these are one and the same. Therefore there are special spiritual properties within all the elements that make up your surroundings and within all the things that you depend on for survival. You can learn to tap these spiritual properties to assist you on your path toward higher centered experiences. This does not mean transcending the physical as your religions have taught, but rather to go deeply within the physical to find the Tao there. Remember that the game on earth is to experience the earth in myriad ways, not to ignore it or try not to be in it.

You have seen that before your human form you experienced the mineral, plant, insect, and animal kingdoms in Devic form. You participated in the enormous creativity of these elementals for eons, helping to form them and assisting them in their growth and evolution. You know these kingdoms intimately and are subconsciously aware of their powers. Yet many of you have forgotten how to speak their language and no longer look to them for their wondrous abilities to heal and balance you as you live.

Minerals, gemstones, plants, and animals all have powers that, if asked for, can dramatically increase your effectiveness in the world. When you become consciously aware of their properties you increase multifold the power that they have to help you.

> For centuries man benefited indirectly from the power of electricity to assist him. Electricity in the form of lightning would start a fire that man would find and use for cooking, etc. When man discovered how to directly tap the powers of electricity his effectiveness jumped a quantum leap.

The elemental kingdoms give of themselves freely and actively have courted man's company for the sake of their own evolution. There is an agreement between the two that states that they will work for the mutual benefit of one another. Due to ignorance and greed man has often not kept his part of the bargain and this throws the natural balance off. When you consciously use the physical kingdoms with mutual benefit in mind you keep the agreement and further the evolution of both.

In this section we will introduce a massive topic. We will explain how you can begin to tap the power of the planetary tools consciously. We will show you how each overleaf has a corresponding gemstone and animal that influences and assists its functioning. You can pull these forms to you physically, figuratively, or symbolically and they will have an immediate impact on your emotional, intellectual, and energetic functioning.

In this fashion you can boost the power of your own overleaves or pull in the power of one you wished you used more often.

> _For example, a king might wear diamonds to boost her mastery or an artisan might wear diamonds to help him be and appear more masterful._

Most important of all however is your natural instinct or impulse to move toward or away from particular gems, plants, and animals. The ones you are repelled by may throw you off balance. The ones that you love will tend to balance you. You naturally know this and tend to regulate yourself subconsciously. When you know this consciously you can more effectively avoid those elements that do not benefit you and draw to yourself the ones that do.

GEMSTONES AND MINERALS

Gems and minerals are perhaps the most abundant tool available to you on the planet. The mineral kingdom includes a rich variety of structures that literally make up the planet beneath your feet. When you realize that your body is also made up of minerals, metals, and transformed earth materials you can see that you can be physically and energetically responsive to these structures around you. The composition and makeup of gems and minerals influences your moods, your attitudes, and your energy level.

Stones in the ground.

There are a variety of ways that the mineral kingdom influences you. Firstly you are constantly being influenced by the composition and nature of the landmass that you live on. You may notice a distinct change in your mood and feelings as you move from one place to another place of different mineral and rock content.

> For example you may live in an area with a great deal of jasper in the ground about you. This influences you to be energetic and lively and you get used to this energetic influence. You may then travel to an area loaded with grey jade, noted for its tension reducing qualities. You will feel much calmer than usual until you leave the area.

Stones you wear

You often subconsciously gravitate to those gems that are naturally balancing or helpful to you. Many times you will pick up a small stone that appeals to you and carry it about for a while. You are usually attracted to that stone for a reason. As mentioned, when you consciously wear a gemstone for its influence you manifoldly increase its ability to affect you.

The most popular way that gems and minerals influence you is when you wear small amounts in the form of jewelry or when you wear them decoratively. Even a very small gemstone can be enough to affect your personal well-being. A small diamond set in a ring will help you to appear and feel more masterful, a kinglike quality. A bit of untreated turquoise, a favorite among Navajo artists, will open you up to the higher emotions.

Historically kings and queens would wear valuable gems in their crowns and scepters. These gems were worn both as an impressive display of wealth and because they actually affected the personality of the person wearing them. The gems helped them to look and be more powerful, inspirational, and just.

Man-made gemstones are also effective as energetic tools because it is the chemical makeup of the gem that creates its energetic properties. They have the added advantage of being much less expensive and more available than some of the rare natural ones. Not all man-made gems however are the same composition as the gem they are supposed to copy.

Some stones and gems are heat treated to bring out their color. This may alter their chemical composition, thus changing their energetic properties. It is best to use untreated stones.

Also it is helpful to realize that gems in their natural uncut state are as effective as cut stones.

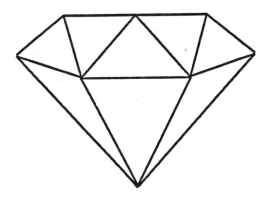

Stones in the environment

Gemstones, rocks, and metals influence the atmosphere of a room when they are used for decoration or when they are used as building materials. Gold gives a grounded mellow feeling to a room (often experienced in churches), while silver lends a high frequency air of buzziness to the setting. Not all gems affect people in the same way. Some are balancing to high frequency people and some are balancing to low frequency people. Some minerals are helpful only to people with certain physical maladies. Here we will not attempt to delve into such a large topic. The chart that follows presents only some of those gemstones that relate to the roles and overleaves.

Keep in mind that you can use these rocks to enhance your own overleaves or to balance yourself with influences that you feel you lack.

> *If you have a goal of acceptance and are having trouble accepting a difficult person you can wear blue-green tourmaline to enhance your ability to accept. On the other hand you may have a goal of dominance but also wish to appear and be more accepting of others. You can also wear blue-green tourmaline for this purpose.*

More information about the healing and balancing properties of gemstones can be found in *Michael's Gemstone Dictionary*.

Roles

Server	Ruby, Purple Spinel
Priest	Light Blue Sapphire
Artisan	Dark Blue Sapphire
Sage	Emerald, Green Spinel
Warrior	Garnet
King	Diamond
Scholar	Yellow Sapphire, Imperial Topaz

OVERLEAVES:
Goals

Re-evaluation	Hematite, Pink Crystal
Growth	Peridot
Discrimination	Smoky Quartz
Acceptance	Blue-green Tourmaline
Submission	Kunzite, Pink Sapphire
Dominance	Blue Topaz
Stagnation	Pink Tourmaline

Modes

Repression	Alexandrite
Passion	Coral
Caution	Citrine
Power	Aquamarine
Perseverance	Jamesonite, Watermelon Tourmaline
Aggression	Fire Opal, Fire Agate
Observation	Clear Quartz Crystal

Attitudes

Stoic	Green Jade
Spiritualist	Moonstone
Skeptic	Orange Jade
Idealist	Lavender Jade
Cynic	Jet
Realist	White Jade
Pragmatist	Golden Topaz

Chief features

These reduce the influence of the chief features rather than enhance them.	
Self-Deprecation	Carnelian
Arrogance	Emeralds, Peach Spinel
Self-Destruction	Amazonite
Greed	Amazonite, Bloodstone
Martyrdom	Amethyst
Impatience	Amethyst, Royal Blue Crystal
Stubbornness	Golden Tiger Eye, Blue Lace Agate

Centers

Intellectual	Amber
Higher Intellectual	Pearls
Emotional	Lapis Lazuli
Higher Emotional	Turquoise
Moving	White Opal
Higher Moving	Black Opal, Sodalite
Instinctive	Bone, Petrified Wood, Mother-of-Pearl

Channeling Stones

	Sugilite, Blue Calcite

ANIMALS:

You co-inhabit the planet with the animal kingdom, whom you have agreed to assist on their evolutionary path. In exchange for your good will the animal kingdom has agreed to assist you in a variety of ways. On the purely physical level animals agree to provide you with food products as well as skins and decorative parts for your appropriate use. Animals offer their labor in exchange for care and compassion. On a spiritual level animals have agreed to provide you with knowledge, wisdom, and energetic assistance for your guidance and inspiration.

Historically man has been aware of the spiritual assistance of the animal kingdom and honored this help through totem worship and the like. Shamans knew how to tap the power of animal species to assist them in curing, finding game, discovering shelter, and learning about weather patterns. The shamans knew that particular animal species were experts in specific areas of knowledge. Birds were the experts on seeing, coyotes knew about cunning and survival, deer were mystics with knowledge of healing and so on.

You, in your evolutionary journey through the animal kingdom, favored certain types of animals, spending more time as an antelope for example than a beaver. As a human you retain your affinity for these animal forms lifetime after lifetime. You can discover this by noticing which animals you love to watch, have around you, and have in symbolic ways such as stuffed toys, ceramic, or wood carved animals.

These animals will be the ones that can help you the most energetically speaking.

For example you may find that you love to have pictures of tigers decorating your walls and statues of them on your mantel. You love watching them at the zoo and always watch animal specials on television about tigers. You can be sure that their constant presence in your life affects you and influences your state of balance positively. Should you feel imbalanced you can consciously look at your tiger symbols with beneficial results.

To gain even more positive results from your favorite animals you can speak to them in a meditative state. One representative is all you need to imagine because your relationship is with the entire species of animal. If you love sparrows, it is the entire species that you love, not just one physical one. You can picture that animal and pose questions that you need assistance with. Simply wait to hear the answers or watch the symbolic gestures and pictures that the animal wishes to show you. Always thank the animal when you are finished.

In addition to your special helpers in the animal kingdom you can draw assistance from animals that are associated with each of the roles and overleaves. Should you desire a little more passion in your life you can imagine, draw, or collect figures of baboons. If you are in school and need to be more scholarly you can work with the image of hawk. In your meditation you can ask hawk to help you see more clearly and improve your study habits more. They are experts in this matter.

When you are dialoguing with animals in this fashion it is not uncommon to have special and even magical chance meetings with them. This is the animals' way of letting you know that you are working harmoniously together. Remember that animals benefit from assisting you and they are pleased that you have requested their help.

For example, if you are attempting to free your emotions and are working with the guinea pig you might strangely find one poking around your back yard one day. You might then spot pictures of them in the oddest places. You will find guinea pigs showing up everywhere.

On the other hand you might find that everywhere you look you see the image of a sloth. This might be an important message to you that you need to slow down and rest more or perhaps go on vacation. The sloth is associated with the goal of stagnation.

The following are animals representing the Roles and Overleaves.

Roles

Priest	Zebra, Flamingo, Llama
Server	Elephant, Pigeon, Oxen
Sage	Otter, Parakeet, Orangutan, Tanager, Oriole, Muskrat
Artisan	Deer, Nightingale, Platypus
King	Bull, Canary
Warrior	Bear, Gorilla, Hummingbird, Woodpecker
Scholar	Hawk, Falcon, Parrot, Cockatoo

OVERLEAVES

Goals

Growth	Fox, Sparrow
Re-evaluation	Elk
Acceptance	Robin, Panda, Bluebird, Finch, Lovebird
Discrimination	Shrew, Hyena, Mink, Toucan
Dominance	Lion, Cardinal
Submission	Ostrich, Mole, Sandpiper
Stagnation	Sloth

Modes

Passion	Baboon
Repression	Whippet, Bird of Paradise
Power	Rhino, Dragon
Caution	Tit-mouse
Aggression	Camel, Goose, Badger, Macaw
Perseverance	Yak, Albatross
Observation	Eagle

Attitude

Spiritualist	Heron, Gazelle
Idealist	Penguin
Skeptic	Puffin, Lemur
Realist	Giraffe
Cynic	Raven, Armadillo, Egret, Porcupine
Pragmatist	Pelican, Seagull, Duck

Chief Features

Arrogance	Rooster, Peacock
Self-deprecation	Skunk
Greed	Squirrel, Bluejay, Crow
Self-destruction	Lemming, Vulture
Impatience	Monkey, Chimpanzee, Antelope
Martyrdom	Opossum, Gopher
Stubbornness	Mule, Buffalo, Bison

Centers

Emotional	
Intellectual Part	Horse
Emotional Part	Hamster, Guinea Pig
Moving Part	Cat
Intellectual	
Intellectual Part	Owl
Emotional Part	Beaver, Raccoon
Moving Part	Rabbit
Moving	
Intellectual Part	Snake
Emotional Part	Cheetah, Mouse
Moving Part	Cricket, Grasshopper
Instinctive	
Intellectual Part	Frog
Emotional Part	Wolf
Moving Part	Tortoise
Higher Emotional	Pegasus
Higher Intellectual	Unicorn
Higher Kinesthetic	Tiger, Swan, Panther

POWER ANIMALS

Power animals and totems are devas who are available as guides and special helpers. Throughout the ages and in all cultures certain individuals have spoken of contact with special magical animals that come from the spirit world to provide assistance to those in the physical world.

These power animals take the form of animals you know—natural animals like the bear, weasel or hawk. Sometimes they can take the guise of magical or mythical animals—Pegasus the winged horse, dragons, unicorns and so on.

Power animals are seen by some as the source of energy and life that sustains them. Witch doctors and medicine men have believed that their healing powers and their powers of sorcery are attributed to their relationship with their power animals.

Younger soul cultures tend to believe that their entire tribe shares the same totem animal. They fear the totems and practice rituals to appease the wrath of the totem animal. Sometimes they are assigned a power animal at birth that will then stay with them until the next tribal right of passage. These cultures tend to formalize their totems and build elaborate rituals and laws regarding their relationship to them.

Older souls begin to perceive that totems are actually personal representations of their own Devic animal experience that they can draw from for assistance and guidance. Each person has had personal Devic experience in each of the kingdoms, mineral, plant, animal and so on. As mentioned earlier some fragments spend a longer time in one kingdom or another and develop certain affinities for one or more species. The pattern of this affinity often follows the pattern of role but this is by no means a rule.

> *For example, remember that those who specialize in Devic experience with birds of prey tend to be scholars, bear specialists are usually warriors and so on. These animals then are frequently your inner power animals. You literally have known them inside and out.*

The power animal can represent an area of accumulated knowledge over many lifetimes. So if you had developed perceptive skills over many lifetimes and needed to get in touch with those powers again on an essence level, you can draw on that sense of perceptivity through the image of your appropriate power animal such as the eagle.

A businessman seeking to close an important contract can develop a daily meditation practice involving the power animal of the fox and the association of cunning. The fox may even tell the businessman what strategies and moves to make.

The power that comes from that animal, the special help that it can provide, comes from its particular talents as an animal. So the excellent eyesight of the eagle gives you better eyesight, better conceptual vision, better perception and so forth. The buffalo can give strong powers of endurance and strength. The fox gives the ability to be mentally quick and a sense of cunning and strategy.

Large animals are not necessarily more powerful than small animals. Many people have power animals such as the sparrow or mouse whose survival abilities are unique and particularly helpful. They show you how to survive when you are not intimidatingly powerful. Compare the nature of the elephant with the sparrow. The sparrow is a bright opportunist, daring and quick. The elephant is slow and lumbering, and historically has spent much time in the service of man as a passive and obedient worker. The characteristics of the animal are important rather than size.

Certain animals are helpful for their physical attributes and the consequences of having special features such as an exaggerated organ or attribute; consider the giraffe for its neck and farsightedness; the water buffalo for its sheer muscle; the rhinoceros for its skin (being like a coat of armor); the llama for nimbleness and so on.

Other animals are helpful for more generalized traits—the cat for grace, relaxation, and speed; the rabbit for fertility; the fox for cunning, the sloth for dormancy.

The power animal can be called upon with an intentional request for help. Occasionally the power animal must first be internally confronted and will appear as a foe or potential hazard. Only after this challenge is met will the power animal become an ally and helper. This is because contact with the power animal is usually made through the instinctive center, the container of all personal Devic experience.

This kind of confrontation often takes place in the dream state and surfaces as nightmares and anxiety dreams. Occasionally the confrontation will be physically manifested.

> *For example you might be frightened or even attacked by a wild boar while in the bush. If you survive the attack you would then be able to use the inner wild boar as a guide, perhaps as a source of strength for withstanding attack in battle.*

The animal represents an area of mastery and accomplishment; perhaps in this instance, being confronted with the vision of your own death, you become a fearless warrior.

Occasionally your power animal can confront you with an intense transforming experience that can herald a change in the direction of your life. The incident may appear like an extraordinary coincidence that impacts your life either directly or symbolically.

These events, then, are synchronistic in nature and sometimes have an air of unreality. The circumstances are often strange or peculiar. You can try to dismiss them as mere coincidence but you will be hard pressed to do so, especially when the same animal shows up in your dreams and your fantasies.

The power animals in these experiences are not individual fragments of the hive souls. The fragments involved represent the entire species—all deer, all bear, all eagles. The inner power animal represents the collective experience of all the animals of that species. This gives them powerful symbolic value and makes them difficult to ignore or dismiss.

In summary you can see see how infant soul tribes used their belief in power animals for growth, and raised their mastery of the environment as well. Power animals played a major part in the development and integration of tribal life and of their

POWER ANIMAL

ultimate survival. Gradually, as these infant souls developed toward baby soul perceptivity, totem ritual became more important and facilitated growth in social consciousness. With the development of civilization and culture and the emergence of young soul perceptivity, power animal consciousness was relegated to myth and was only hinted at in the names of athletic teams and automobiles, and in metaphors. Respect for animals was lost and they were seen as something to confront, dominate, harness, or kill. Their spiritual value was forgotten and their potential as internal guides and healers was ignored.

Mature soul perceptivity has begun to remind humankind of its relationship to the animal world by attempting to save species from extinction and launching an environmental awareness.

Old soul perceptivity has begun to remind the planet of the spiritual value of the animals.

In modern society you have lost the structure that integrates the significance of animals in our lives. This discussion seeks to bring to life the ways you can relate more closely to the animal world in an intimate, personal and powerful way. It offers an alternative to the current philosophy that gave rise to man becoming the dominant species on the planet, seeking to kill off animals for the more simplistic needs of food, survival and territory. On a deeper and more subtle level the same applies to plants and even ultimately to rocks and minerals and water and air. What is needed is to evolve philosophy and practices that integrate man with the planet on every level.

PART THREE

BALANCE AND HEALING

Chapter Six

Healing and Balance

Part III: Balance and Healing

In this section we will cover many aspects of the healing process including tools you can use and steps you can take to promote balance. We pay particular attention to the healing power of dreams and how to maximize their healing potential. We will review the seven major chakras, describe how they are structured, and discuss how you can work with them. Then we will discuss the centers in relationship to the chakras and show you how you can become imbalanced through the functioning of the traps of the centers. We will demonstrate how you can work with the centers to heal yourself energetically, intellectually, emotionally, and physically.   At length we will examine the importance of the instinctive center and how you can work with it to discover balance and healing. Finally we will show you how *the negative poles of the goals and modes lead to imbalance and how you can work with each of them to heal yourself.*

THE ELEMENTS OF BALANCE AND HEALING

The first pictures that come to mind when we speak of healing, are typically, cultural versions of curing the sick. While recovery from illness is certainly part of the healing process, we want to expand the definition of healing to include all efforts to balance the imbalances that occur in every area of your life, energetic, intellectual, emotional, and physical.

How do you become imbalanced and why do these conditions exist? One way you have explained this process to yourselves is through the concept of original sin. "Someone must have done something wrong way back in the beginning somewhere, to account for all the imbalance and suffering in life. Somebody [Adam and Eve] must have been bad and you must pay for their transgressions", you might say. Within this context you think of illness as punishment and healing as being saved or forgiven. Now this is understandable for infant and baby souls as an explanation for the karmic nature of life and its resolution. However, there is another more accurate version of imbalance and healing that is a more appropriate explanation for older souls at this time

Remember that the way the physical plane is set up, you play the game of learning by constantly moving among the three poles of the triad, positive, negative, and neutral. You swing from positive to negative or vice versa until you eventually find neutral.

For example, you are deliriously happy about a new found relationship [positive], then you see all its flaws [negative], then you find a sense of equilibrium about it and accept its positive and negative aspects [neutral]. You could call this a balancing act that repeats itself over and over again in all areas of life.

Healing, then, is finding the balance or the neutral position of acceptance. We could therefore say that all of life is truly an attempt at healing. This is the way you set up the game in the first place. Imbalance is created by you deliberately, so that you can rediscover the Tao through attempts at balance. This is the cosmic game of hide and seek that on an essence level you said you wanted to play. You can forget about all those tales about a fall from grace and being bad little boys and girls, because that explanation gives you no respect and no responsibility for setting up the whole challenge of learning with intelligence.

The truth is that you learn the most about yourselves and about life on Earth from falling off balance, then finding your way back to balance again. When you are out of balance, then you experience the negative poles of your overleaves. When you get back into balance you experience the positive poles of your overleaves. Since the negative poles and the positive poles are two sides of the same coin, disease and healing are also two sides of the same coin. You cannot have one without the other. They are inseparable.

The day you have nothing more to balance, no more karma to redress, no more concern with learning on the physical plane, is the day you are ready to cycle off. This is the natural graduation of every fragment that passes through the soul ages and levels of the physical plane.

So given the nature of imbalance and healing, what can you do to become a more effective player, better at remembering who you are? How can you become an efficient healer for yourself and a catalyst for helping others to find balance? The answer is one that you have heard many times before. Unconditional acceptance is the cure for all disease and the basis of all healing. It speeds up the learning process and reduces the experience of pain. Remember that there is no value to pain and suffering unless it leads to some kind of learning. If you learn what you want to learn then you can dispense with the suffering. Eventually you will learn how to learn without suffering at all. That will be a day for a party. Now, an additional word about agape or unconditional acceptance is in order here. Recall that unconditional acceptance is not the same as giving up or feeling hopeless. It is the understanding that ultimately, anything that happens is all right. It is also the acceptance of whatever issue caused the disease in the first place. That is what brings in the neutral position and helps you find balance.

Who Heals.

Ultimately all healing is self-healing because all healing is determined by essence, not by personality. Your personality, although it forgets sometimes, cannot heal itself without the assistance of essence. If your personality is not aware of essence, it feels that it must do all the work itself. When it does get a sense that there might be an essence running the show, personality becomes fearful because it really isn't sure whether this is supportive or a threat to its own survival. If it perceives essence as a threat, then it slides into its negative aspect, the false personality made up of the chief feature and the negative poles of your overleaves.

When this happens, false personality can even block the healing of essence for a time. False personality frequently develops its own agenda. For example, it may serve the chief feature of martyrdom by hanging on to an illness long after its potential for growth has been used up. The false personality can fight off essence attempts to heal for a time, but essence always succeeds because it has an infinite supply of time and resources on its side. Personality simply cannot heal itself without the assistance of essence.

Essence can block attempts by others to heal the personality, if the lesson of the experience has not been learned. On the contrary, essence often allows another fragment to assist in the healing process because much can be learned from this kind of relationship. This healing relationship often satisfies karmic debts and fulfills the healer-healed monad. If you become imbalanced emotionally due to faulty beliefs, then essence may arrange for you to work with a counselor who owes you a karmic debt. That counselor may have made you crazy in a past life. Now, that same fragment is eager to help you find sanity.

If you are a person who finds fulfillment in the healing professions, then you would do well to understand who you can heal and who you cannot or should not heal. First of all you can never help to heal someone who has not given you permission to do so. This permission need not be given verbally, but of course this helps. Using your powers of visualization you can ask that person on an essence level, whether healing or balancing is appropriate at this time, whether you are the right person to help, and if so, what methods would produce the best results.

Blind attempts to heal everyone and anyone often result from the chief negative feature of arrogance. Out of a fear of personal vulnerability, you compensate by trying to heal the whole world. This gives you the illusion of control and invulnerability. Healing of this nature is largely ineffective because it is not being sourced by essence but by the fear in the personality.

If you wish to become an effective healer, then your motivation is sourced from an essence level. You can detect essence motivation by its unconditional nature. Thus, true healing is a result of agape.

Healable and non-healable states of imbalance.

How can you tell if your state of imbalance in any arena is healable or not? You may say, "Why should I bother trying to cure myself of cancer if essence wants me to have this problem". Or you may say, "I am going to see with my eyes again no matter what, even though my optical nerves have totally disintegrated". Sometimes it is difficult to separate out the wishes and wants of personality from the serene voice of essence. The best way to accomplish this is to quiet the intellectual and emotional centers through meditation and in silence, allow yourself to know the truth. Sometimes the truth is not black or white.

For example, essence may resist your attempts to heal a state of imbalance until you have learned something important from the experience. You may need to listen to what essence wants you to learn. If you get the lesson sooner than later, you can then heal yourself right away. If the lesson requires six months of experience with the problem, then you best cultivate some patience and understanding.

Essence will always speak the truth if it has a forum. That forum is created by a desire to know the truth and a time of silence. This is why silent retreat is such an important form of healing.

You can know whether another person's state of imbalance is healable or not through a similar technique.   Relaxation, quieting the emotional and intellectual center, and visualizing the healee is an effective method to know more about the true nature of their condition.

THE FOUR MAIN AREAS OF DISEASE AND HEALING

Mental imbalance and healing: Intellectual center

Firstly, you can become imbalanced mentally or on the level thought and belief. When your beliefs become overly developed to the detriment of other beliefs you are in a state of imbalance. For example you may believe that you are not intelligent enough to be promoted in your job. The more powerful this belief, the less influential are more moderate beliefs like, "I can learn what I need to."   This level of imbalance can rather quickly effect the emotions, and if not corrected, eventually creates physical symptoms as well. Mental imbalance can go undetected for a long period of time because it masks itself with rationalizations and other mental defenses that make the imbalance appear normal. Eventually negative beliefs and obsessive thoughts become so disturbing that they cry out for healing.

Mental imbalances can be created by essence for the purpose of having particular experiences. These types of mental imbalances will resist all attempts at healing until the experience is complete.

Most mental imbalances can be healed by insight and emotional processing of the fear attached to the belief. Almost all mental imbalances are interrelated with fear. Dissolve the fear and balance the mind. Hypnosis, concentration, study, and re-education are some of the chief methods for working with intellectual imbalance.

Emotional imbalance and healing: Emotional Center

Secondly, you can have an imbalance occur emotionally which is one step more physical than your belief system and your chakra and energetic make up. Emotional imbalance usually occurs only after you have neglected to alter your beliefs or you have not corrected a chakra imbalance for awhile. Here you are overcome by an excess of a certain emotion such as anger, sadness, or frustration and you feel off-balance. Your emotions directly affect your ability to function normally and you may withdraw from your regular life activities. Every part of your life can be affected by your emotional state.

Becoming aware of emotions and honestly communicating and airing feelings toward others is healing and balancing to the emotional center. Past life regression or remembering the source of difficulty in childhood can be helpful. Color, art, and music can be valuable in the healing of emotional imbalance.

Keep in mind that when working with emotional release, dramatic expressive displays are not always helpful because often they serve as a mask for deeper, unexperienced feelings. Artisans and sages and those similarly imprinted are capable of avoiding true emotion in this fashion. The key here is the visceral response in the solar plexus and not the more superficial emotive expression.

Energetic imbalance and healing: Moving center

Thirdly, you can have an imbalance occur energetically, through the underuse, misuse, or overuse of one or more of your chakras. This is a non-physical level of imbalance that, if discovered in time, can be corrected fairly quickly through energetic processes such as meditation, focusing, concentration, mind control, and exposure to certain smells, colors, and music. If you have an imbalance energetically you may not immediately notice it unless you are highly sensitive. It may show up as a feeling of tiredness or having too much energy. You may feel overly closed off to other people or perhaps too vulnerable.

Energetic imbalance can have several sources. You may become energetically imbalanced by the chronic beliefs that you carry. For example you may believe that there is no such thing as an essence and that spiritual life is pure fiction. Through this belief you shut down many of the channels of communication between your essence and your personality. Many of your chakras shut down, opening only in high stress or emergency situations.

Energetic imbalance can occasionally be produced by outside interference such as allowing-in the negative thoughts of other people or by attempting to perform certain spiritual exercises when one is not yet ready. For example, a baby soul practicing voodoo or black magic can become energetically imbalanced from these practices.

Energetic healing and balance results from many of the exercises already mentioned as well as visualization, meditation, chakra balancing, spinning, and hypnosis. Sometimes the skill of a healer is necessary to assist with energetic imbalances.

Physical imbalance and healing: Instinctive center.

Fourthly you can have a physical imbalance that can be diagnosed as a disease or illness. Your temperature, blood pressure, heart beat, and functioning of bodily organs are affected and their ability to do their job is curtailed mildly or grossly. Physical forms of imbalance, are created externally by trauma to the body [karma] or internally by chronic belief patterns.

As with the other areas of imbalance, physical disease may be chosen by essence for specific lessons, and therefore, render healing attempts fruitless. Although the personality can sense this at a basic level, it sometimes resists the disease process intensely, creating much additional suffering and obscuring the value of the experience.

> *For example essence may allow the personality to contract an incurable disease because it sees that the personality needs to learn about compassion for those with similar health problems. The personality can deny the lesson and pretend that nothing is wrong or it can desperately cling to a variety of ineffectual remedies without learning anything.*

Often imbalances are created by essence for specific learning experiences. For example essence may choose to alter the instinctive center for life so that it operates in a highly imbalanced way. The imbalance of the instinctive center can effect the chemical balance of the body in such a way as to produce severe disorientation, hallucinations, and delusions. Essence may choose to prevent the healing of these disorders until a particular experience is completed.

When instinctive healing is desired by essence, in addition to those processes already mentioned, it can be brought about by intense desire, visualization, and the psychic intervention of an able and experienced healer. Often you will need to include a physical form of healing as well, in the form of diet, herb remedies, rest, and occasionally surgery.

THE HEALING PROCESS

It is important to realize that all healing techniques whether they be physical, energetic, mental, or emotional are an attempt to re-establish proper flow.

Blockage or stoppage has occurred because somewhere, somehow there has been limited perception. The direction of healing then always moves from the more limited picture to the big picture, from the personality to the essence.

The key behind all healing techniques is intention and focus of attention. Since energy follows thought, all dis-ease is a product of certain thought processes and healing is the result of certain balancing thoughts. Thoughts without the energy of emotion however are not result producing. Here's how it works.

The thoughts are sourced in several ways. First of all, there are thoughts created and delivered by your own essence meant to communicate to your personality certain insights about the nature of its actions. Secondly there are thoughts produced by your non-physical helpers and spirit guides that are meant to influence your actions and reactions. These include the devas of plants, animals, minerals, and elements. These kinds of thoughts are delivered through your various overleaves into your personality via the chakras and the centers.

There are also collective thoughts, mass produced by your species, that form invisible clusters. These accumulated thought forms are magnetic in that they tend to attract thoughts that are similar in nature to their main theme through their principle emotional content. Likewise they are attracted to people who are having thoughts that are like them. They then add to the intensity of the thoughts with their own mass. These kinds of mass thoughts are drawn through your chakras, instinctively by you, to influence your overleaves.

All of these kinds of external thoughts tend to be laden with their own kind of emotion. For example, thoughts about killing someone are usually laced with fear and anger. Thoughts about helping someone usually carry the emotion of love and nurturance. These emotions are the glue that hold the thoughtforms together

Your personality chooses which of these external influential thoughts will influence your own thinking and feeling. The more allied with essence is your personality, the more you choose to attract thoughts commensurate with its motivations and the greater your ability to rebut thoughts and emotions of a negative nature.

To the extent that your chief feature runs you and you operate out of false personality, you fall prey to the influence of thoughtforms created by others' chief features throughout their lifetimes. Some of these thoughtforms have become so large and massive that they have been represented as demons and evil spirits by baby soul religions.

>_For example, you are in a foreign city and you are lost. You must ask strangers for directions. In one scenario you feel confident that anyone you ask will be friendly and helpful to you because you have been operating out of the positive pole of your goal of acceptance. As you generate the initial thought it is immediately joined by the energy of similar thoughts and feelings of those that expressed similar ideas. This bolsters your original notion and makes it highly probable that you attract a stranger that is friendly and helpful._
>
>_However, let us say that you have been habitually allowing your chief feature of martyrdom to influence most of your waking thoughts and ideas. As you approach others for directions, you have the conviction that you will be given the wrong directions or that in some way you will be victimized by them. This immediately attracts all thoughts of a similar nature permeated with fear. The original conviction is thus strengthened making it more likely that you will attract someone who does victimize you._

It is important to remember that these collectives are actually neutral in that they have no volition of their own. They are purely reactive and influence only when they are drawn-in so to speak. Fear tends to attract the more negative thoughtforms such as the lust for war whereas love tends to attract thoughtforms more associated with essence goals.

Some thoughts are created by the negative poles of your own overleaves and by your chief feature. These are the thoughts of your false personality. Whatever their source, your overleaves take those thoughts and generate energy that adds to the emotional content of those thoughts. This energy is propelled outward by means of your sensations. This is the way you create and resolve your karma.

Dis-ease happens in a two step process. First you suppress the activity of your overleaf and misdirect the energy being produced there. Secondly you suppress the misdirected energy and you become physically ill.

For example, you suppress your emotional center expression and misdirect this energy toward lets say your moving center. So instead of feeling your emotions you are driven to act them out instead. But then you suppress this energy as well because it might get you into trouble. You then get physically ill.

Lets say you are deeply disappointed at having been passed over for a promotion at work. When you get home, you don't want to express your grief to your family because you have been enculturated as a man to be strong and show no weakness. On impulse you decide to go running instead but then you stub your toe on your way out the door and you squelch that idea. With no outlet whatsoever, your immune system is overwhelmed by the toxins created by stress. You fall ill with a virus that was formerly latent in your body.

You have a thought that to express your emotion is possibly dangerous to your status as a loved husband and father. This thought effectively blocks energy and emotional expression. Healing here, means feeling the permission to express the emotion without the danger of rejection. Thus healing is restoring proper flow.

Permission is a directed thought delivered with compassion. If this is received, healing can begin.

Let us say however that instead of suppressing your emotion, you act it out in some indirect fashion. Instead of communicating your disappointment over the lost promotion, you go running instead. This is still unbalancing because you are trying to make one center do all the work for another center. Your moving center cannot take over for the work of your intellectual and emotional centers. You may end up physically tired, but you have not necessarily altered the thoughts and feelings over the event. What is necessary here is the thought that you are still loved and the permission to express the grief that you feel through talking and if necessary crying.

If, however, during your run you manage to work with your thoughts and gain insight into the big picture reasons you chose to be passed over, you begin the process of healing. This can give you the permission you need to express whatever regret you still carry.

SOME STEPS TO SELF HEALING.

1. Being present

The most important element of self healing is the ability to be present with yourself. You cannot begin the process of self healing while you are preoccupied with mulling over baggage from the past or actively scripting the future. These activities scatter your focus and energy to the effect of rendering you powerless to alter your state. When your focus is blunted and your energy is dissipated by mulling and scripting you lower your natural frequency in a way that makes you slow to respond. This often shows up as the pseudo emotion of depression or the non-emotion of apathy.

The path of healing requires your reorientation and focus on the present moment of aliveness. However, focusing on the present brings up the true emotion that was being masked or blocked. This usually represents experiencing painful feelings before the release to joy. Therefore it is usually avoided.

Being in the present moment means facing the pain that is based on fear. However being in the present allows you access the higher centers for energy and support that was formerly blocked. So, as you face the fear, you become privy to a most powerful set of supports that exists within you at all times.

To become present, pay attention to the sensations in your own body. Since your body is always present, you will be guided by it to be present also. You may not however, like how it feels. It may be angry with you for abandoning it or it may be petrified with fear. This you must face if you desire healing. In the event you are in so much emotional or physical pain that you find it impossible to be present, then you need the support of another who can help you to become present more gradually. After all, after a long absence, becoming present can be a shocking experience.

2. Grounding.

One excellent method of becoming more present is the process of grounding your energetic system to your immediate locale. since your body is presently residing on the planet Earth, the Earth is the most expedient place to ground to. Here is how it is done.

a.   Relax by sitting and sighing deeply several times.

b.   Imagine a connection between the base of your spine, general area of your instinctive center, and the core of the earth.

c.   Strengthen and clear this channel by following it slowly down and then up, once again using the power of your imagination.

d.   Use this channel to drain away excess energy and any unwanted condition. Send it downward for recycling.

e.   Next, concentrate on energy from the earth rising through openings in the soles of your feet, up your legs, into the base of your spine, and distributing gradually throughout your body. Since the Earth is always present beneath your feet, it will have the effect of immediately bringing you into greater focus through your body.

3. Establishing an Essence connection.

After you have established a sense of grounding to locate and stabilize your body, you are in a position to bring into it a higher degree of essence. Bringing in greater degrees of essence accelerates spiritual growth and awareness and promotes healing on every level.

Whereas it is not possible to squeeze the totality of your essence into your physical body, most people bring into their bodies only a fraction of the essence potential available to them. You can raise this amount with an act of will and concentration. However it is important that you do this incrementally to avoid overwhelm. Your body, if habitually subjected to low levels of essence and energy, may regard increase of essence within it, as an intrusion and a threat. It must get use to the increases gradually just as you must introduce food slowly after a fast to avoid nausea.

Otherwise the body will react in fear and resist essence expression.

Here is a method to raise the level of essence within your body.

a.   Imagine a ball of brilliant energy, perhaps eighteen inches over your head. Postulate that this represents the totality of your essence, pure potential and infinite energy.

b.   Imagine that through a hole in the crown of your head, you could draw a brilliant beam or channel of this energy down into your head; gradually streaming through your head and face; down your spinal column, branching through your arms and out your hands; cascading down to the base of your spine meeting the upwelling earth energy there. Create a mix and distribute this mixture gradually throughout your body.

c.   Expel the excess energy and unwanted conditions through the base of your spine down into the Earth.

d.   You have mingled essence here with the physical material that forms your body and comprises your personality. This is the marriage of the Sun and the Earth. The child is you.

e.   As you reach greater levels of comfort with practice, bring in more and more of each stream until you ar working with large amounts. Expect an emotional, physical, or psychological reaction, so do this slowly over a period of days and weeks or even months. Several times a day for five minutes or a longer sitting of twenty minutes is sufficient.

f.   The increased streams of energy tend to dislodge blocks and obstacles within your energetic system. As they are dislodged and removed they come to the surface, so to speak, for review. You need not become overly identified with them, a simple acknowledgement will do. However, as these come up, there is a tendency for you to feel that all these old problems have come back to plague you. Many people discontinue the exercise at this point because they fear it is making them worse. Understand that this is part of the process. Presently you will feel better than you ever have before.

g.   You may experience physical reactions such as trembling and shaking. If these become too uncomfortable, discontinue and breathe deeply a few times. Bending over from the waist and touching your toes, without locking your ankles can be of some help.   This helps to unblock the joint chakras and dissipate the accumulated energy. If you experience intense physical pain during the exercise, you are most likely trying to go too quickly. Discontinue for the time being and slow down.

h.   This method was known to Egyptian spiritual practitioners who derived the technique from earlier forms used in Atlantis.

4. Calling for support.

Power animals and helpers from the other planes are an important part of any healing process. Although all healing is self healing, you do not exist in a vacuum. You are intimately related to members of your entity, your essence twin if you have one, and the many teachers, friends, and students you have developed over your lifetimes. These relationships exist whether they are in physical form or not. When they are not in a physical body, they are in a unique position to help from within, because they are not distracted by the many challenges of the physical plane.

Therefore when you feel overwhelmed, ill, or imbalanced in any sort of way, it is appropriate to ask for help and support. You may not, however, have your lesson removed or resolved for you. What you get is perspective and guidance. The work remains yours to carry out.

To get acquainted with a spirit guide, follow the steps outlined in the section on spirit guides. To enlist their support, do the following:

a.   Ask for a spirit guide whom you know and trust or one that is an expert in the situation you are trying to heal. Ask and you will receive.

b.   Ask them to help you with some of the healing steps we have outlined so far. Ask them to help you with staying present, grounding, pulling in higher degrees of essence, clearing your aura and so on.

c.   Ask them to help you with insights or clarity concerning the condition of imbalance.

d.   Always remember to thank them for their help. Do not be concerned about directing their activities or taking charge of the healing operations. If you wish them to move out, simply state this

5. Bringing in the higher planes for healing.

When you have learned how to bring higher degrees of essence through your chakras and into your body, you have developed the ability to work with the higher planes.

ASTRAL PLANE: Provides help in the form of power animals, devas, and some guides that can offer support and guidance of a more practical nature. Help with emotions.
CAUSAL PLANE: Provides teachings and philosophies of a higher order similar to this teaching. Help with beliefs.
AKASHIC PLANE: Provides information about past lives, parallel lives, and future probabilities. Instinctive center healing.
MENTAL PLANE: Higher intellect. Intuitions about the nature of the universe. Understanding connectedness with all things. Perceiving the truth.
MESSIANIC PLANE: Higher emotional. Perceiving the nature and feeling of agape or unconditional love.
BUDDHAIC PLANE: Higher Moving. Perceiving and experiencing the nature of energy. Understanding beauty.
TAO: Connecting with all that is.

To contact the other planes for healing, all you need to do is to acknowledge them and ask to feel the energy of that plane. It helps to visualize the chakra that you wish to bring it through. For example, for a condition of severe self deprecation or depression, you may wish to visualize the fourth or heart chakra. Establish a connection from this chakra to a color or symbol of your own choice for the messianic plane, center for higher emotional healing. Channel the energy of agape from the messianic plane through the fourth chakra, for a period of one minute or less. A little bit of healing from these planes can go a long way.

If you are seriously ill or wounded you may wish to hook up your third or solar plexus chakra with a symbol for the buddhaic plane, center for energetic healing. Again, you need not hold the connection for longer than one minute.

You can see then, how you can use each plane for healing in its own specific area. The upcoming section about chakras will explain which chakras to work with.

Very occasionally you may wish to connect with the Tao through the crown chakra on the top of your head for a few moments. This will give you a spiritual healing of the highest order. This is the healing of choice at the time of death.

In order to accomplish this, follow the same procedure described above. Visualize a symbol or globe of brilliant white light for The Tao. Draw a channel between that light and the crown of your head. Funnel that light into your crown for a few moments.

6. Healing with your hands.

Your hands are magical instruments in that while they are quite physical, they have astral properties as well. This is because of the chakras that exist in the palms and at all the fingertips.

Your hands then, are able to mold and direct energy just as they are able to mold and direct physical matter. They are most useful tools in the art and practice of healing. Your hands work in harmony with your intent and your will. Therefore whatever you intend through your thoughts and feelings can be channeled through your hands. This is the process behind the ancient art of laying on of hands.

Do not hesitate, then, to use your hands in self healing or when you assist another. Use your imagination and concentration to direct light and color to different parts of the body and through the various chakras. Use your hands to help the flow of energy through the joints or for clearing obstacles from the aura. Use your hands for soothing or for closing down that which is gaping too wide. Use your hands to send away unwanted thoughts or to help bring in desired beliefs or feelings.

Placing your hands over physical wounds has powerful healing properties. Unfortunately because of your cultures fixation on germs you have been instructed to keep your hands away from injured parts. While it is unwise to touch a gaping wound, it is certainly helpful to pass the hands over it.

Many a doctor, masseuse, dentist, and even palm reader has effected healing through touch without the conscious knowledge of it.

7. Steps to healing others.

Remember that all effective healing is an attempt to help people heal themselves.

1. The first step is to establish communication with the healee mentally and emotionally. Note that they need not be present physically for you to accomplish this.

    If they are not present physically it helps to know their name, age, sex, and their address or location.

2. Establish a communication link with their first chakra (instinctive center). Greet them and ask their permission to work with them. Ground them and bring them into the present.

3. Assess the problem by posing questions and viewing the mental image pictures you receive. You may sense these instead of see them.

4. Attempt to see, sense, or feel the problem through the eyes of the client. Walk in their shoes for a moment without identifying.

5. Focus your attention on the area of difficulty, not with the intention of increasing its strength but with the intention of understanding it more completely.

6.   When you get a sense of the problem and have assessed it to your satisfaction, begin to use practical images to heal the malady. For example, if something is separated, use tape to fasten it together. If something is bloated or too full, open a faucet to drain it. If something is leaking, cork it up. Use your hands even if you are alone.

7.   Next, channel healing energy from the various planes, not from your own personality. The best way is through inspired feeling and images of brilliant light. You can both visualize this and direct it with your hands if you wish.

Any tools or steps that you used for self healing can be applied to others. If you wish, with their permission, you can channel higher degrees of their own essence into their chakras or into their crown. You may wish to show them how to do this for themselves.

Chapter Seven

Tools for Healing

EXTERNAL TOOLS FOR HEALING

In the process of healing you may wish to bring in added tools from the environment to assist with balancing. Some of these tools are spoken about in greater length elsewhere in this book. You may wish to look over the section on tools of the planet to give some ideas about healing tools. Here we are simply going to list some of the categories that you may wish to draw from to assist you.

Keep in mind that in each category are elements that have an imbalancing effect on the person. You can use your perceptions to determine this. What is unbalancing for one person may be balancing for another. The examples we have listed here have a universally balancing effect.

*

Mud of various mineral contents for a variety of conditions. Smearing on parts of the body and covering the entire body. Drainage and extraction. Unplugs.

❂

Heat applied to body or body parts. Viewing flame is healing to the cells. Restoring and soothing. Promotes energy flow.

Plant substances taken externally and internally. Too many to list in this work. Their preparation has every thing to do with their effectiveness. Simply viewing some plants and being in their vicinity can have powerful healing effects.

While certain plants have universal properties that affect most people the same way, many affect people differently. To find out, simply ask the plant or flower and sense the response. If you are still in doubt, run your hand or hands over it and then ask. This will help to bring in the information.

❀

Flowers are universally healing in their effects. Viewing and smelling flowers is the most effective in healing. However some of their properties may be extracted for oils and applications on or in the body. This is the subject of an independent work. Again, ask internally for their unique properties. Some may be unbalancing for certain people.

Power spots and ley lines. Natural locations in the land
that promote cellular repair, energetic repatterning,
and emotional balancing. Can be determined through
intuition and a natural impulse to go there when you
are imbalanced. You may be able to sense them
through your hands or solar plexus.

They are often publicly acknowledged places of
pilgrimage or known for their healing properties.

Art and shapes. Viewing art and geometric designs can
have enormous healing effects. Viewing the circle or
mandala is universally balancing. Being in a circle or
circular structure is even more powerful. Triangles
increase energetic instability but provide interest.
Box shapes are beneficial for organization and
structure. Ragged shapes can be unbalancing.

Smells of various planetary objects have a healing
nature. The smell of many kinds of animal dung has
beneficial and balancing effects. Think of the good
feeling that results from being near or around stables.
Consider the smell of the sea, the smell of flowers,
seasons, forests, and rain. Soothes, energizes.

Likewise certain smells can have an imbalancing
effect. Consider the noxious smell of automotive
fumes.

Running water or moving water has powerful balancing
properties. Being in it or near it is best but simply
viewing it from afar or hearing its sounds is
beneficial. It has the effect of uncorking, draining,
opening.

✤

Cloud viewing has a most healing effect on the psyche.
Essence expression becomes more possible from this
exercise. Good for almost every kind of malady.

➡

Wind can be both balancing and imbalancing depending
on season and location. You will know by the effect it
has on your psyche. Harsh, steady winds are best to
avoid. Brief turbulent winds and gentle breezes are
usually best for healings.

❀

In some cases, chilling or extreme cold can have
beneficial effects on the body.

Minerals and metals affect the body in a great variety of
ways. Crystals etc. See tools of the planet.

INTERNAL TOOLS: THE HEALING POWER OF DREAMS

You use dreams in a great variety of ways to balance you and
set up conditions for healing. Dreams are for the most part,
actual and real experiences that are roughly remembered in a
symbolic form when you awake.   Here we will discuss how
dreams are used by essence to arrange your reality and set up the
conditions you are seeking.
First we will list the different categories that dreams fall
into and then we will discuss the healing properties of dreams.

1. Past life memories: Some dreams are exact memories of
past life events that are karmic in nature.   That is, they are
intense events that are in some way incomplete or unfinished
within your psyche. They show up in your dreams, often in a

recurring fashion, because they are pushing for some kind of resolution in your present life experience.

For example, you have a recurring dream that you are falling from a horse. As you fall, you feel that you are encased in metal and you experience terror and wake up in a sweat. This is a past life memory of a death experience from fifteenth century England. You were in fact falling from the back of the horse you were riding while wearing bulky armor. The weight of the armor brought you down and that ultimately caused your death at the hands of enemy soldiers. That life you had a chief negative feature of stubbornness just as you have in this life. The stubbornness then, led you into the situation that caused your demise. If you had been more flexible, you would have tried to negotiate with the enemy before drawing your sword.

Now, although you are not a soldier and conditions are somewhat different, you are in a similar pickle. Due to your stubbornness, you are headed for a run-in with your boss, a conflict that could cost you your present job and livelihood.

Now, it so happens that your boss was one of the enemy soldiers that killed you. This represented a karmic payback for an earlier situation when you caused his death in a raid on his village in what is now Southeast Asia. Thus the karma is resolved. You are now testing yourselves to see whether the lesson has been learned. Will you create the karma again, or have you learned another way to resolve the difficulty between you?

Your essence is attempting to get your attention by showing you the ultimate results of your past folly, falling to your death. The dream, of course, makes you sweat, as it is meant to.

The way you can tell a past life dream of this nature is that the details of it are clear and distinct, and are repeated exactly the same way each time you have the dream. These dreams universally have a healing intent. They are always meant to get your attention to a problem area.

Sometimes these past life recollections are combined in symbolic form from several lifetimes to represent a single theme needing attention.

> *For example, you may dream that large turtles are drifting over the sands away from you. You try to catch them but they all disperse and you feel sad and desolate. A group of men come up to you and tell you to get out of there. They threaten you with sticks but you draw a line on the dirt and they cannot cross it. You feel anxious and pull out a fan and begin to fan yourself. You at once feel better.*

The dream sequence combines experiences from three different lifetimes, all related by theme. The turtles are a memory of a life in the South Pacific where you were unsuccessful as a hunter and you were considered a failure by your tribesman. The group of men are a memory from an aboriginal life on the continent of Africa where you were abandoned by your mother and adopted by a neighboring tribe. You were never fully accepted into their clan because of your difference in appearance and eventually because of your negative behavior you were driven away to a life of hunger and eventual starvation. The fan is a memory from a life in China where you were born a deformed girl, but by the kindness of a midwife, you were allowed to live. She brought you up and you eventually found a niche in society as a skilled animal trainer.

All three memories incorporate the theme of ostracism and rejection. The final memory however, recalls a successful adaptation and mastery of the theme. Since you are now struggling with rejection in several current relationships in your life, the dream sequence recalls similar past events and a past success in handling rejection.

2. Shaped dreams: Shaped dreams represent ongoing work on an unfinished past life situation or current event. They tend to be problem solving in nature and represent development of a theme.

> _For example, in the falling dream mentioned earlier you eventually dream that you fall off the horse but you are not encumbered by armor. You bounce up and engage in a kind of jig with others that suddenly appear. You wake up feeling serene and calm. This dream sequence represents further development of the recurring nightmare. Here you are working out negotiations with the so called enemy and by dancing with them you find another set of results. You are no longer encumbered by the hard armor symbolically representing your chief feature of stubbornness._

The nature of these dreams is change. There are new situations and new characters in each dream.

Often the shaped dream is a collaborative effort on the part of all parties involved. You may meet nightly to learn a group lesson or shift an impasse among you.

3. Converging vectors: These dreams prepare you for contact with an old friend or past life associate. These dreams appear vague or more traditionally dreamlike in that they do not conform to your notions of reality. They tend to be more symbolic. Remember that they are preparatory dreams and are not the actual contact itself. They are a kind of dress rehearsal for the actual drama of meeting. Therefore you do not see their conclusion or final result because by nature they are open ended.

These vector sensing dreams are the products of choice and are never accidental. They do not represent mere wishful thinking but are actual plans being made.

4. Astral travel: If you are a mature or old soul you have most likely developed proficiency at astral travel during your sleeping hours. Here you travel on an essence level, out of your body to visit with your task companions, essence twins, friends, relatives, and other karmic relationships that you are involved with. During these actual nocturnal meetings, you make plans and choices about upcoming events in your physical waking hours. You may arrange a chance meeting with a friend that will begin the process of healing an old wound between the both of you. You make plans to complete karmic ribbons, fulfill obligations, offer support, and initiate projects of all kinds.

The hallmark of these travels is a sensation of flying and repetitive patterns of contact. That is, every time you meet with a particular individual, the pattern of contact will be the same.

> *If you are meeting an entity mate or cadence partner who happens to live a continent away, you will always greet each other the same way. Perhaps you will always see them salute in a unique fashion or they will be wearing the same costume or outfit. This is your sign to one another that the contact has been made. The messages or information you exchange will change each meeting, but the initial contact will remain the same.*

Many of these travels involve learning, just as you learn during your waking hours. These you often remember as having attended classes or meetings of one kind or another. If the meetings are regular, there will be a repeating symbol associated with them.

How to Work With Your Dreams for Greater Power and Healing.

The more you become consciously aware of your dream experience, the greater your ability to take advantage of its

33232222

healing properties. You can heed warnings more rapidly, understand obstacles more thoroughly, and initiate positive actions to accelerate your growth. Here are some simple steps to maximize the potential of your dreams.

1. Pay attention to your dreams. To help you remember them, clear out the days accumulation of worries with a light meditation. Clear yourself with flourite, sage, or a warm bath. Tell yourself firmly before you sleep that you are going to remember your dreams. When you awake, try not to move your body before you have recalled what you were dreaming. Write down any scraps or fragments of dreams immediately when you awake. Continue to do this until your recall has increased.

2. Identify the type of dream you have had, based on the categories we mentioned. Was your dream a converging vector, an astral sequence, a past life recall?

3. Pay attention to details within the dream sequence. What were you and others wearing? What was the mood or feeling? Was there a sense of familiarity or was the experience bizarre and unfamiliar?

4. Reflect on the characters in the dream. Do they in any way feel familiar? Do they remind you of someone you know or once knew?

5. Re-dream the sequence in your awake state. Play with different outcomes. If there were no conclusion in the actual dream, give it one to your satisfaction. What happens after the monster lunges for you and you woke up? Carry the sequence out. Face the fear and go beyond it. If need be, allow yourself to be torn apart and eaten by the monster. After all, these are your dream images and you can do whatever you want with them. Do you become the monster then? Perhaps the monster transforms into a friend.

6. Interview the characters in your dream. Ask them who they are and what they are doing there. Have them dialogue with each other. The secret again is to play with the images. When you play with the images you actually alter the reality of them. You shape your reality just as you shape it in your sleeping state. Do not fear that if you explore negative possibilities that you will bring them about. What turns a dream image into physical reality is intention and desire, or conversely, resistance to it.

7. Regard your dreams as helpers and healers no matter how unpleasant or uncomfortable they make you feel. They are served up by your essence via your instinctive center to help you progress and evolve either by processing unfinished business or by creating new strategies.

Try to validate your dreams whenever possible by checking with friends if you have had a dream about them or by following the impulses presented to you within the dream. Discover for yourself the intimate relationship between your dream sequences and your apparent waking reality.

SOUL AGES AND HEALING.

Soul age is not exactly a tool for healing but it is a context through which healing may occur. Healing will appear dramatically different throughout the different souls ages. There are five soul ages that are experienced in a physical sense. They range from infant to old. Two other stages, transcendental and infinite, are rarely experienced in a physical body. Each soul age has seven levels each requiring at least one and usually many more lifetimes to complete. Each level has a theme and a particular lesson. For a more complete description of these levels, consult The Michael Handbook. Here is what you can expect to see in both the healer and the healee within each soul age.

Infant soul:

For infant souls, healing is mostly survival. To be healed means to stay alive. Infant souls are not experienced enough to feel imbalanced in their chakras or even in their emotional states. If they are severely disturbed, they have little to compare this condition to. Therefore, they are happy just to stay alive long enough to accrue some experience.

Infant souls tend to be quite superstitious and can find solace in the belief that evil spirits have been warded off or that their enemies have suffered at the hands of their rituals.

Infant souls often resort to revenge to feel emotionally released from grief or the pain of loss. They tend to find release in acting out any emotion such as anger and finding an immediate target for it.

As healers, late level infant souls can be effective as shamans for their tribal groups. They would not function as healers in larger more culturally diverse centers.

Baby soul:

Baby souls seek external forms of healing for all categories of imbalances. If they are emotionally upset, they desire medication or pills from the doctor. If they are frustrated they tend to funnel their feelings into somatic symptoms and complaints. They push for surgery to cut out the offending organ rather than attempt to address the belief or attitude that is at its source. This is the same level of response that you would find in a toddler. A two or three year old desires relief from pain and discomfort, not insight. The small child looks to the parent for solace and expertise when they are ill.

Thus baby souls place heavy reliance on the authority of the doctors and medical experts.   They are often healed with placebos.

Baby souls do not often seek the role of healer. When they do, they approach the profession like they approach everything else, with tradition and orthodoxy.   They will tend to treat conditions exactly the same way according to a recipe or they will tend to see conditions in terms of polarities. If a person is good and obeys the rules, they will not fall ill. If they are bad, they will fall ill.   Dis-ease and illness is often seen as punishment from God for wrongdoing. Thus patients are often treated with some distaste and judgement.

Young soul:

Young souls vary according to whether they are early or late in their cycle. Early level young souls tend to act more like baby souls in that they lack insight into their own healing process. They prefer to see imbalance as coming from external causes and seek help by external application to reduce symptoms. Late cycle young souls begin to give lip service to internal causes. They are more likely to see that some of their dis-eases are a result of stress in their lives and they may adopt measures to reduce that stress. Unfortunately, many choose alcohol and drugs to mask symptoms and end up addicted. Young souls tend to be impressed by the healers status, credentials or high fees. They usually seek out the experts in the field, the best that money can buy.

As healers young souls have a tendency to divorce the person from the symptom. They talk about a person as a schizophrenic in ward #6 or a case of aids in room #43. The challenge of healing is directed toward finding a cure rather than relating to the individual.

Young souls as healers are more focused on the power that comes with the healer role. Many young souls choose psychiatry and medicine because of the prestige and high pay that your culture bestows on these professions. Some do reasonable jobs as technicians but they do not comprehend the internal nature of illness and imbalance. Nor do they understand the true nature of the healing process because, to do so, robs them of the importance they bestow upon themselves.

With young souls in dominance within the healing arts of your culture, medicine has become big business and technology substitutes for true understanding. Notice that, with the shift from young soul to mature late this century, the medical establishment is faltering, on the verge of a total collapse. Look for the closing of hospitals and centers of traditional healing. Look for the establishment of smaller community based healing arts centers relying on both traditional and non-traditional methods.

Mature soul:

Mature souls begin to grasp the true nature of the healing process as we have been describing it. Since mature souls are in great internal stress, they are more apt to seek psychological and emotional help than any other soul level. They seek understanding and some measure of relief from the psychic pain they are prone to. Because mature souls are deeply emotional and focused on relationships, they are more likely to experience imbalance emotionally in the context of relationships. Often they enter into long term intense relationships with the healers they seek out. As they get older in soul age, mature souls are more likely to experience frustration with young soul oriented healing methods and instead seek out unusual and non-traditional forms of healing.

As healers, mature souls tend to make excellent emotional contact with their patients and clients. They display a much greater sensitivity and understanding for the internal pressures and motivations of their healees. Often they enter the field of healing to ultimately seek answers and heal themselves.

Mature souls tend to be intense and serious about their healing practice. They are not able to achieve the detachment and big picture perspective that comes with the old soul cycle.

They take their patients seriously and stay up nights worrying about them because they identify with their pain.

Mature souls fight for patients rights and become advocates for the helpless and the infirm. They can become quite angry with the mercenary focus of big business and medicine, often volunteering their time or working long hours for low wages. They have recently graduated from young soul lives wherein they, themselves practiced such mercenary approaches to healing. They feel a desperate need for balance.

Old soul:

Old souls tend to be practical as patients. If they are break a leg they go to a good technician to have the leg set and placed in a cast. If they have a sore throat, they are more likely to fast and take herbal remedies than see a doctor. Old souls have a tendency to try to handle most medical problems themselves if they can. They may even try their hand at stitching up a cut themselves rather than going to the hospital.

Old souls recognize the inner nature of imbalances and seek to redress these at their source rather than at their symptom level. They tend to see injuries as opportunities for lessons or as choices they may have made on an essence level. They are more apt to see the karmic or self karmic nature of imbalance. Sometimes they are overly hard and ruthless with themselves with regard to these. They will be unsympathetic to what they see as their own childish needs for attention or rest.

They seek out assistance when they are frustrated with their rate of progress or when they feel so blocked they feel depressed or discouraged. They readily respond to insight and spiritual motivation.

Old souls are most likely to seek help by going out into nature or seeking out who they perceive as a true healer, whether credentialed or not. They are not particularly impressed by high fees or licenses.

As healers, old souls often select the non-traditional route. In cultures that require it, they may seek out the easiest route to legitimize their practice whether it be a ministers license or a degree in psychology. They tend to develop a relaxed detached, approach, giving lip service to the cultural rituals and expectations, while practicing their own brand of healing. On occasion the patient may feel they are not being taken seriously enough. This is because the old soul has a difficult time seeing the immediacy of the pain, preferring to look at the big picture instead.

Old souls place emphasis on educating the patient to heal themselves and let go of reliance on the practitioner. When they are dealing with much younger soul ages, they may experience a great deal of frustration with the dependency and worship of their patients.

Finally, old souls are difficult to peg regarding the fees they charge for their services. They tend to make up their own rules and ethics regarding the payment of such fees. They may see someone for free and charge another person a hefty fee. They do this according to the needs of their patients and their own needs to make a living. They have become more detached tending to see money as an exchange of energy. Their attitude is that it all works out in the end.

THE ROLES: ESSENCE TOOLS FOR HEALING

There are seven essence roles, one of which makes up your primary beingness. You choose your role for the full cycle of lifetimes and develop it to maximum potential by the time you are ready to cycle off the physical plane. You will find a brief description of each role in the appendix, The Michael Teaching in a Nutshell or see The Michael Handbook.

Each role makes a contribution to the healing process in its own unique way. Likewise certain roles are more prone to imbalances in certain areas than others. Each role then has its strengths and weaknesses both in terms of personal imbalance and healing and in the way they assist others to heal. Here we will describe in limited terms some of the characteristics of each role with regard to healing. Then you can identify with your own role and begin to work with your limitations as well as increase your effectiveness as a healer.

Warriors

Warriors have the best sense of grounding and physical balance. They are in touch with their bodies and familiar with its condition. Because of this and their keen ability to focus, they tend to rapidly physically heal. On the other hand they tend to be the roughest with their bodies and can abuse them a great deal.

As healers, warriors can be effective because they are able to focus and are not easily distracted by surrounding events. They communicate a sense of groundedness and make the other feel that everything is under control. Their maternal approach communicates safety and nurturance. Because their positive pole is persuasion, they can literally persuade the healee to take more care of themselves and become balanced more quickly.

Warriors as healers, can become overly heavy handed with those that they are trying to assist. When the healee feels bullied or pushed around it rouses their resistance and this is usually counterproductive. Staying in the positive pole is the key for warrior healers.

Kings

Kings, like warriors, are in touch with their physical bodies. They are slightly better at avoiding some of the physical damage that warriors can accumulate. Because kings are mastery oriented, they do not put up with imbalances that last a long time. This makes them rapid healers, but at the same time can make them extremely difficult patients when they cannot master the illness right away. They become tyrannical and difficult to please. On the other hand, they are good at galvanizing others to help them and they tend to end up with plenty of assistance. Nobody wants the king to be sick. Heads may roll, so to speak.

The great contribution of kings as healers is that they communicate hope. When a king is present, expectations rise because there is a feeling that anything can be mastered, even the most difficult conditions. Rather than personal healing, the king's strength lies in creating a larger context for healing. Their great attention to detail and feelings of overall responsibility make them great administrators or organizers of healing centers and their staffs.

Servers

Servers often feel that they don't have time to be sick and they are often right. Because they are geared toward serving others, they are not prone to illness in a physical sense. However, when they do become imbalanced they have trouble because they are not often good at serving themselves. They will tend to try to keep on serving others until they are too sick to carry on. They do not know their own needs as well as they know others needs.

Servers are the best at making people feel that they are going to be healed. They have the great power to inspire belief in others. They are the best caregivers, nurturers, and support givers. They take care of all the little details in a nonintrusive way and they communicate that they actually enjoy the care giving. This relieves the healee of the guilt over being a bother or being a burden on others. Servers give support by literally being in charge of the healee.

They like to take control of the healee's personal needs and in this way they relieve the patient of the burden of many personal details. On the down side, this, if carried out too long or exuberantly, can make the healee dependent or malingering.

Priests

Priests on the average run an extremely high frequency of energy and this mitigates against physical illness. On the other hand they are more prone to energetic, emotional, or intellectual types of imbalance. Priests can become way off balance because they are like violins, needing to be finely tuned to sound good. Their rigid missionary zeal at times can cause them to neglect themselves until they are completely run down and out of balance. They are usually moving so fast that they do not make good patients. They do not see themselves as needing help but rather as the ones that are needed to help others.   If they have fallen ill or imbalanced, they take off at the first opportunity they can get back on their feet.

Priests are healers in the large sense in that they inspire others always to see the bigger picture. They are excellent at getting others to see the source of their illness and how their illness fits into their life's journey.   They are also excellent at pointing the healee toward the support available from greater sources, essence, spirit guides, and the Tao.   Priests are able to channel large amounts of energy that can be used for healing purposes. They are particularly good at laying on of hands and prayer as a vehicle for healing.

Priests inspire and heal through their presence alone. Often just a visit from a priest can start or facilitate the healing process. They are good at communicating to the healee their own sense of power and compassion.

On the down side, priests can become overly strident, rigid, and zealous in their approach, driving the healee away in the process. The healee may feel blamed, inadequate, or punished for being ill. Shifting to the positive pole of compassion is the resolution. It is perhaps more important for priests than any other role to keep themselves in balance. An imbalanced priest can wreak havoc. A balanced priest can accomplish a great deal. In order to remain balanced, a priest needs to be willing to slow down and focus on self for periods of time. Priests often need to reduce the arrogance that can build up over the lifetimes of authority and being in the public eye. They need to realize that they are not always right, sometimes their own backyard needs attention.

Artisans

Artisans have the advantage of being emotionally expressive. When they allow their creativity and expression to flow, they seldom fall ill. Of course when they dam it up, they are prone to indescribable moodiness and can be quite adept at manufacturing new illnesses. In fact artisans are responsible (not in a negative sense) for creating all illnesses because they are, after all, the inventors.

When artisans become emotionally or mentally imbalanced they manifest the most bizarre and extreme symptoms. They can be the craziest of the the crazy. When they become physically ill to the point of self destruction, they can create tumors and cancerous growths galore. On the other hand they are just as good at making them disappear to the great frustration of the medical doctors.

Artisans tend to be visionary masters and as such, have great ability see the healing process from a bigger picture perspective. They are excellent at creating healing meditations, rituals and ceremonies and are the inventors of many devices and new technologies that can aid in the healing process. Because they are so adept with their hands, artisans make excellent surgeons and dentists, working with flesh and bone as they would any other artistic medium.

Sages

Because sages like to have fun, they are less inclined to become sick or stay sick unless there is something valuable to learn from the process. On the other hand they can be incorrigible when healing requires rest and silence. Many a healer has thrown up their hands in exasperation as their sage patient with the broken leg pranced about the room in an animated display of how it happened.

As a group, sages have perhaps the most most healing quality of all and that is the special ability to bring humor and fun to the situation. Throughout the ages, clowns, comedians, jesters, and entertainers have facilitated countless healings and balancing for others on all levels, physical, emotional, mental, and energetic. Children particularly respond to the healing of sages and sometimes their presence is all that is required to turn the tide from illness to health.

Sages heal through their wit and their words, through poetry and prose, through their facile ability to turn despair into hope with their creative expression. They are the best at moving people from the negative poles of their overleaves to the positive poles through their humor and story telling abilities.

Scholars

Scholars, being the eclectic role, can display a range of all the behaviors we a have been thus far describing. Because of their assimilative nature however, scholars tend to display more illnesses and symptoms than any other role. They are sponge-like and absorptive, desiring to record all events and all information they come into contact with. Often they are indiscriminate about what they absorb. They are particularly prone toward clogging or blockage because they absorb and store better than they eliminate. In fact scholars hate to let go of anything they have accumulated because this feels unnatural to them. This continues until the scholar finally learns that all experiences are being stored energetically in the akashic records and need not be stored in the physical body. This tends to be an old soul realization.

Because scholars have tremendous curiosity, they tend to try a great many experiences that others would prefer not to. A scholar may try out a strange disease or imbalanced condition just to see what it is like.

As healers, scholars are the most knowledgeable about healing tools and techniques. They store a vast library of information about healing herbs, plants, and minerals, and know what their best applications are for. Because of their neutrality and ability to get along with every other role, they are particularly good at working with many kinds of people, even the more difficult kinds of patients.

Scholars act primarily as mid-wives, helping others to contact their own information for healing purposes. They frequently occupy the position of shaman or medicine person for their tribe or community.

Their challenge is to communicate empathy and compassion for the injured party. Because of their reserved expression, their bed-side manner can occasionally be too cool and detached for the patient needing warmth and caring.

Chapter Eight

The Seven Chakras: Healing and Imbalance

Each one of your overleaves or personality traits affects, and is affected by, one or more of the seven principle chakras or energy centers along the spinal column.   These chakras are thrown off balance by negative pole activity in your overleaves. They are brought back into harmony and balance by positive pole responses of your overleaves. Thus, for example, if you have a goal of growth and you act out of the positive pole, evolution, you will balance and heal your sixth chakra. If you slide into confusion, the negative pole of growth, you will throw your sixth chakra wide open into overwhelm, or you may completely shut it down in protest.

Here are the seven chakras and the principle areas that they govern.

The Seven Chakras

7. Crown chakra at top of head,   Spiritual wisdom, higher intellectual.
6. Third eye at forehead.   Perception, intuition, higher emotional.
5.Throat. Communication, discrimination, creativity,   intellectual center.

4.Heart
      Affinity, self esteem, agape, acceptance, emotional
    center.

3.Solar Plexus,
      Power, control, competition, energy distribution, moving
    center.

2. Abdomen,   Sexuality, basic emotions, higher moving.
1. Root at base of spine.   Survival, past life information, instinctive center.

HOW CHAKRAS FUNCTION

As you may recall, the chakras are non-physical bridges between the personality and the essence. They act like communication links delivering information about the state and condition of the body to essence and in return they issue forth wisdom from essence to personality. The chakras are formed on

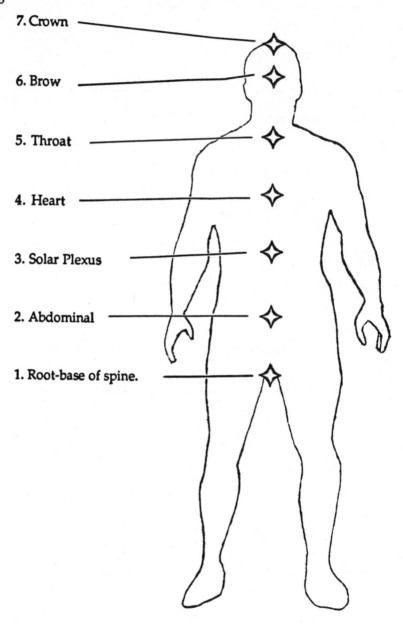

7. Crown

6. Brow

5. Throat

4. Heart

3. Solar Plexus

2. Abdominal

1. Root-base of spine.

the astral plane and occasionally can be seen by the physical eyes by fragments gifted with higher sensibilities. Emotional centering usually helps with this.

The seven chakras are shaped rather like discs of vibrantly spinning colors. They tend to open and close similar to the way an iris in a camera opens and closes to allow in more or less light through the aperture. The chakra closes tight when it is shut down and opens wide when it is active and filled with energy.

Each chakra is also a storage center of information related to certain functions that the chakra governs. For example the fifth chakra in the throat area, has much information about communication and expression. The nucleus of the chakra has the basic information about how it functions and this core should almost never be altered during a healing process. The core of the chakra is surrounded by seven layers. Each layer holds a record of all the information gathered during an entire soul age. For example the first layer around the nucleus of the chakra has information about all the experiences gathered during the infant soul cycle related to that chakra. So, for example, the third chakra in the solar plexus, related to power issues, records all the learning that the person has accumulated from having power mode and the goal of dominance plus any other experience of power during the many lifetimes of the infant soul stage of development. The second layer relates to the baby soul age, the third to the young soul age, the fourth to the mature soul age and the fifth to the old soul age, and so on.

If a person has not yet experienced a soul age, that layer lies latent, not yet filled with information. By looking at the layers of any chakra you can determine a fragment's soul age. The chakras of younger souls are less developed and simpler than the chakras of older souls.

Seven Layers of the Chakra

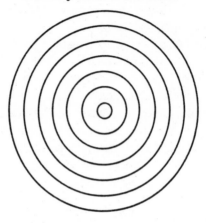

CHAKRAS AND SOUL AGES

INFANT SOUL CHAKRA: Small, undeveloped, Basic information about survival. Little information stored about overleaves.

BABY SOUL CHAKRA: More dimension than infant soul. Boxlike. Some stored information about overleaves.

YOUNG SOUL CHAKRA: Added dimensionality. Layered. Nut-like.   Considerably more sophistication.

MATURE SOUL CHAKRA: Many layered.   Multi-dimensional. More challenge to heal because more complex. Deeper and more inter-relationships.   More resistance to healing than old soul.   More flexible however than younger souls. Tent-like, flexible.

OLD SOUL CHAKRA: Increased dimensionality yet paradoxically simpler in organization. Easier to work with than mature soul chakras because more flexible.   Responds more quickly to healing. Fluid.

WORKING WITH THE CHAKRAS

The chakras are a complete record of all the knowledge a person has gained about overleaves from all their lifetimes. An older soul has lots of experience and can refer to a wealth of information about the appropriate use of a particular overleaf. A younger soul may have nothing to go on and therefore bumbles along less appropriately with a current overleaf.

The topmost developed layer of the chakra is a record of the current lifetime experience. As with the other layers, this layer is subdivided into many other layers, each depicting a year of life, something like tree rings. To determine the source of a particular problem you can count the number of years back to the place where you see the energy blocked usually by a dark spot or a blotch in the normally beautiful color pattern.

For example, using the power of visualization, you may wish to see the source of a problem in your own or another person's chakra. Let us say you are working with a mature soul who has a communication block. They are afraid to speak in public.

1. First you look at the topmost part of the fourth layer of the fifth chakra. This is their current life experience. You can blow this layer up in size so that you can determine the exact year where the problem began this lifetime. You count back and see that there is a discoloration twenty five years ago when the person was seven years old.

2. You focus on that spot and ask to see the mental pictures recorded there. You see that the person was humiliated in class by a teacher in the second grade. The person made a decision at that time that they would never trust speaking in public again.

3. Now you can look further and ask more questions. For example, you may want to ask whether this event had a karmic history. You can then go to earlier layers of the chakra and see the pictures that describe the karmic ribbon resulting in the current life's obstacle. Or you may see associated events in other lifetimes that contributed to this intense difficulty in the current lifetime. If you are not particularly visual you may hear, sense, or feel the information instead.

4. You can sense connections to the activity of the other chakras as well. For example, you may see connections leading to fourth chakra blockage. As you look more closely you find that you closed down and blocked love for yourself and others based on the decision to avoid speaking in public. There is a way that you punish yourself for that decision. So the investigation may lead you to do some clearing and balancing here as well.

Conscious awareness of these events can be helpful to the you. But the true value comes from the emotional completion of the unfinished ribbon or pattern being played out. Complete emotional expression through tears, rage, or laughter is an important part of the healing process.

CHAKRA CONNECTIONS

Now in addition to layers of experience within each chakra, there are potential connections between each chakra and every other chakra. For example, the fifth chakra has a connection to the third chakra and the fourth chakra as well. The third chakra in the solar plexus communicates power and energy to the fifth chakra in the throat. This way verbal communication becomes powerful and influential. The fourth chakra in the chest gives affinity and feeling to fifth chakra communications making them more loving.

These connections are like energetic blood vessels that link the chakras together in a communication network. The basic pattern or blueprint of this network is already formed within each fragment. However this does not mean that it is actualized in everyone. The job of lifetimes is to activate the communication network and realize its latent potential.

Younger souls often operate with their chakras in isolation. They have not yet learned to activate the channels between them. For example, it is common for an infant soul to use the power and energy of the third chakra without any fourth chakra (heart) influence. Over lifetimes of experience, the connection between these two chakras is developed, and information begins to flow back and fourth.

When the network is fully realized in the older soul ages, the fragment becomes so in tune with essence that creating karma is no longer possible. That signals the end of the cycle of lives on earth.

Healing the connections

These channels of communication between chakras may become blocked by habitual thought patterns, conditioning, or traumatic events that cause a fragment to choose to shut them down temporarily. Because of this, even an older soul may feel cut off or experience a fogging of their awareness. These blockages are subject to clearing and healing. It is important to make the distinction between a person who has simply not developed the connection and a person who has the connection but has a blockage there.

You will not be able to heal a person who does not have the experience or development in the area you are attempting to work with. You cannot necessarily heal a person of the desire to kill

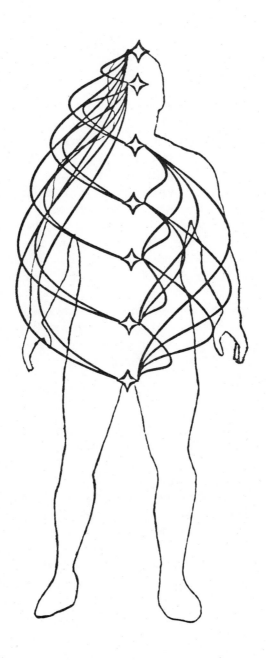

by working to clear their heart chakra. You had best keep them isolated from others and educate them in civilized behavior. This will help them to develop their fourth chakra and curb the third chakra.

The most simple method of knowing this is to close your eyes and mentally ask whether this condition is healable or not. Listen for the answer in your mind. At first you may feel that you are imagining the answer but this is alright. This is natural and you will eventually learn the difference between wishful thinking and an inner sense of knowing. They feel quite different and you will soon learn to tell the difference.

The second way to tell the difference is to use your powers of visualization and see whether the connection is there and whether it is blocked or not. Knowing where to look is the sign of a good healer and you will develop this with practice if you wish.

If you see that a connection exist between for example, the fourth chakra (heart) and the fifth chakra (throat), then you can see where the blockage is and what it looks like. If you wish to know more about it you can pose the question. What is the nature of this blockage? How did it get here? How long has it been here? Is it amenable to clearing?

Blockages are often held in place by instinctive center or first chakra instructions, something you will be reading more about shortly. It is important that you not attempt to remove something that the healee believes is keeping them alive somehow, no matter how misguided. You will have to do some mental communicating with your subject in order to release the fear that is held there. For example the person may believe that if they communicate their feelings, they will be beaten and isolated from the love they feel is necessary to sustain them. They do not realize that this is an old program and that there are other sources of love now, years later.

If you have successfully communicated with the healee and have received permission to clear the block, you can proceed by once again using your powers of visualization to do so.

If you understand your own energetic system and know how to use your own chakras, you can mimic clearing motions with your hands over the spot you are working with. Then you can mimic reconstruction of healthy channels there.

You can act out the healing in a kind of pantomime if you wish. This is effective because it involves your moving center as well as your emotional and intellectual centers. This is particularly effective for the expression roles of artisan and sage because their need to express their creativity. Remember that movement of the hands is especially important because of the chakras in them. These are a powerful healing tool for any role.

OTHER CHAKRAS

There are many chakras beyond the seven principle ones located along the spinal column. Each joint of the body has a mini chakra and there are active chakras in the palms of the hands and souls of the feet. Chakras can be found in each of the inner ears, in the kidneys, and in the fingertips. These chakras are more like energetic bridges, connectors, or links than storehouses of information. For example, the chakras in the palms of your hands are the links between your main chakras and the work you are doing with your hands. Therefore, as we have mentioned, your hands can become powerful channels or tools for healing. This is the basis of the age old knowledge of the laying on of hands.

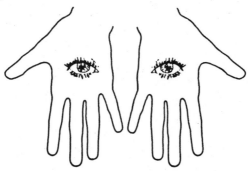

The spinal column is the main trunkline of connections between the seven principle chakras and their connections between all the other minor chakras. These communication links can look like fine hairs or threads emanating from the spinal column like a cloud and encircling the entire body to form an aura. The threads emanating from the first chakra tend to end close to the body forming a first vital layer of the aura. If this vital life layer appears gray, muddy, or dark, the fragment is seriously ill and may be approaching death. Occasionally you may see this condition in someone who appears outwardly healthy. This is often the case when, due to a choice on their part, they are close to physical death of an accidental nature. Only upon receiving news of their death, do you realize why they looked so grey when you looked at them energetically.

The threads from the second chakra form the second layer of the aura, the threads of the third chakra form the third layer outward, and so on. The seventh chakra (crown) forms the outermost layer of the aura around the body.

You can use this aura and its layers to assess a person's relative health and condition. As usual, this takes a lot of looking, sensing, and feeling, as well as some posing of specific questions.

If a layer looks dark or tarnished in a particular area you can trace this condition to its source in the chakra in question. You can then discover whether the source has past life connections or is based on events earlier this life. You can check for karmic threads and begin to understand the nature of these events.

You may wish to assist the person to clear the blockage by mentally infusing the area with brilliant light. See the color returning to the area and the energy beginning to flow. Even more effective is to have the subject join you in this mental exercise. If you wish, you can join with a group in this endeavor, a move that will greatly amplify your power to create the desired change.

Imaging color is effective when you are directing the light. Colors represent different frequencies of light and, as such, they are useful for different applications. White light is not advisable for all conditions because of its intensity. Healing with white light can remove the lesson that is being learned through the imbalanced condition. If this is the case, the person will most likely recreate the condition all over again. Color on the other hand facilitates the accelerated learning of the lesson. If you go about white lighting everything, you are simply delaying your learning through experience.

Here are some general properties of colors when used in a healing capacity:

FOR PHYSICAL PROBLEMS:
Reds are effective for organs, endodermal tissues, and those parts of the body involved in supply and maintenance. Great for the instinctive center and the first chakra.
Greens are effective for muscle, bone, blood, and rebuilding damaged areas. Greens help those areas of the body engaged in supply and distribution.
Blues are effective for the brain, the nervous system, eyes, ears, and all the communication systems of the body. Excellent for the fifth or throat chakra.
Gold and silver generate energy and raise frequency. Gold is more soothing. Good as a healing agent in all chakras. Silver is more glitzy, can be good in the third and fifth chakra.
Pinks and roses are healing for emotions. Excellent for the fourth or heart chakra.
Purples and lavenders are good for spiritual crises. Use these on the upper four chakras. The lower chakras will find this frequency too esoteric. They need the more basic colors. Reds, oranges, yellows.

Browns are excellent for grounding, when the person is spacy or lacking focus. Brown is also a good color for removing the stress of being in the public eye. After teaching or public speaking, it can be soothing. It tends to decord and disconnect one from all the interested parties.
Oranges are good for healing sexual imbalances and energetic conditions.
Yellows are effective for mental confusion and difficulty with the intellectual center.
Clear white light for crises or extremely severe conditions. It clears out everything and creates a condition of starting over. Note that clear white light is not recommended for every condition. After all, you do not give a blood transfusion for every little scrape or abrasion.
Use transparency for cloaking, creating a valence, or becoming incommunicado.
Black and grey are not recommended colors to heal with.

With experience you can begin to know how the chakras work together and how they interface with one another by seeing, sensing, or feeling the relationship between them. You need not always understand everything about a condition before you can be effective at clearing it. The most important thing here is to know whether you have permission to assist with any change. Just because you see the value of a change, does not mean that your subject wants it. Those of you with an attitude of idealism, a mode of passion, or a role of priest or server, need to exercise more restraint in these matters.

Chapter Nine

Balancing the Centers

The centers govern your reaction or immediate response to all situations in your life. They roughly correspond to the function of the seven chakras, although they more accurately represent combinations of them. The centers are the set of overleaves that directly connect you to your own essence. They act as a kind of bridge or pathway between your personality and the source of your being, your soul, or essence. They translate information back and forth keeping your essence informed of your physical experience and communicating essential directives and guidance from essence to personality.

As with all the overleaves, your centers each have a positive and a negative pole. Positive pole reactions lead to health and negative pole reactions lead to ill health. When the centers are out of balance due to negative pole reactions you experience discomfort, illness, or disease. When they are in balance due to positive pole responses, you feel smooth, healthy, and energetic.

No center is capable of sustaining you on its own. The centers depend upon every other center to provide you with your overall living experience. After all, you cannot live on pure intellect, or pure emotion, or pure kinesthetic action. You require a balance of these centers to make you healthy.

When one center is developed and used more compared to the other centers, you run the danger of becoming unhealthy physically, energetically, emotionally, or intellectually.

Therefore we cannot speak of the centers in isolation from each other when we speak of matters of health and illness. Let us see how these centers interact with one another. To begin with, there are seven centers, three lower centers, one neutral or instinctive center and three higher centers.

+ insight	+ perception	+ productive
INTELLECTUAL	**EMOTIONAL**	**MOVING**
- reasoning	- sentimentality	- frenetic
	+ aware	
	INSTINCTIVE	
	- mechanical	
+ truth	+ love	+ integration
HIGHER INTELLECTUAL	**HIGHER EMOTIONAL**	**HIGHER MOVING**
- telepathy	- intuition	- desire

THE THREE HIGHER CENTERS

Let us begin in descending order with the higher centers first. These exalted centers are called upon temporarily in states of spiritual insight and peak experiences. They are not daily experiences for most people and their purpose is not to carry out survival activities in the physical world. Their negative poles do not make you feel bad or uncomfortable. They are simply narrower bands of an expansive experience.

Although you don't live on a daily basis out of these centers, they can occasionally be enormous sources of healing for the mature and older soul levels. Very young souls have trouble accessing the higher centers and when they occasionally experience one, they can be so terrified that the healing potential is negated.

Except for a few advanced level souls, most people are learning to balance the four other centers because they are much more related to the daily affairs of running a physical body, dealing with karma, and living in society with others. Therefore these are the centers we will concentrate on here.

THE THREE LOWER CENTERS:

The vast majority of people tend to react from one of three lower centers, intellectual, emotional, or moving. So, when presented with any situation, your first immediate response will tend to be either thought, feeling, or action. This represents the center that you habitually rely on. If you tend to react with a thought, we say you are intellectually centered. If you tend to respond with a feeling reaction, we say you are emotionally centered. If you tend to react with instantaneous action, we say you are moving centered.

The neutral or instinctive center is so important to the healing process, that we have devoted an entire chapter to it alone.

THE TRAPS OF CENTERS: Imbalance and healing.

You will tend to respond out of these three centers in a specific order. So, if you are intellectually centered you will first react with thought, then perhaps your emotions will follow, and finally you will act. If you are emotionally centered you will feel first, then you might act, and perhaps think about it later. You may have any combination of these three as a habitual pattern based on your most developed center which comes first, and your least developed center which comes last.

This then is the pattern of your imbalance. The closer you come to operating simultaneously out of all three of these centers, the more healed you will be. Too much imbalance causes discomfort and suffering, and may result in emotional, physical, or energetic distress. This, we will look at more closely as we focus on the order in which you react from your centers.

The center that you respond with second, is a key to your state of imbalance. Often your immediate response will be cut short and you will move on to the second center response and remain stuck there. Your third center response ends up coming much later if you ever get there at all. It is because of this second center trap that you become sick or suffer ill health.

There are six possible traps and yours will be based on how you are centered.

Intellectual center first---emotional trap.	Moving last
Intellectual center first---moving trap.	Emotion last
Emotional center first-----intellectual trap.	Moving last
Emotional center first-----moving trap.	Thinking last
Moving center first--------intellectual trap.	Emotion last
Moving center first--------emotional trap.	Thinking last

Let us examine these one by one to see how you can run into imbalance and then get out of it.

Intellectual center first----emotional trap

Imbalance

Here your fifth chakra is well developed and you tend to immediately try to figure things out. You especially are good with explaining things rationally and you use words rather well. So far so good. After you have had your initial thought in response to something mildly stressful, like for example a phone call about a new job, you begin to feel something. However, because your fourth chakra is not as well developed, your first chakra opens and you get stuck in worry, anxiety, depression and obsessing instead of truly feeling full emotion. It is important to realize that this trapped state is not truly thinking nor is it actually pure emotion.

Finally, because your third chakra is relegated to last, you can't seem to get going or take action in the situation. So it would seem that you can not do anything right from this trapped place.

Healing

What to do! For this pattern you need to concentrate on developing the ability to experience a full emotional response at the right time, that is, when the situation is happening. This means learning to regulate and open your fourth chakra appropriately so that it is not stuck at a low r.p.m. for a long time and too late. Meditations on the fourth chakra are helpful as well as listening to music and exposure to beauty in nature or art. Relieve the pressure from your thinking process by giving your emotions something to do. Get them off your thoughts for awhile.

Learn to keep your thinking process clean and pure. Stay with your thoughts until you have insight. If you are concentrating on justifying or rationalizing, you are on the wrong track. You want to truly understand, not engage in an intellectual cover-up based on fear.

Likewise the third chakra needs some energizing and exercise.   Physical work is especially helpful as are concentrations on the third chakra. You will find that when you act, you will move toward healing and away from your trap.

Intellectual center first---moving trap.

Imbalance

Again as above, your fifth chakra is accessible and you react to your experiences by thinking about them first. You are articulate and logical in your approach to life. However when presented with a stressful situation you often find that your thoughts begin to tumble past each other in a never ending stream, giving you hardly a chance to stick with one before you are off on another tangent. Your thoughts seem to race and you are driven to obsessive actions to handle your anxiety.

Here your first chakra drives your fifth chakra and eventually your third chakra, so that you begin to act to control or discharge your racing thoughts. Your fourth chakra emotions are unavailable to you so that you act literally without knowing how you feel. Others may find you coldly rational or robot-like wondering where your sensitivity is. This is an exceptionally uncomfortable state of affairs yet at times you do not even know it.

Healing:

What to do! You need to learn how to move appropriately so that your actions are not reactions based on fear but are right for the situation you are presented with. You need to keep your thinking process clear and uncontaminated with the urge to race on and on. Give your intellect a task to do such as remembering the lines to a song while you work out vigorously. You are in great need of exercise and real physical body motion, not just mental motion. When your mind begins to race you are neither truly thinking nor truly moving.

Likewise your fourth chakra needs attention. When you allow yourself to truly feel emotion, your anxiety will diminish and you will feel more human. You need music, art, beauty and full expression of emotion to help you move away from your trap.

Emotional Center first----intellectual trap.

Imbalance

You are a perceptive person quick to cry, laugh, anger, or feel any emotion that comes. You are quick to like or dislike and you have an ample appreciation for art and music. However, because you have been taught to mistrust your emotions, you have learned to quickly nip them in the bud and think about them instead. So you endlessly wonder over and over why you felt the way you did when you responded to a situation emotionally. You feel that you have to give reasons for your emotions but try as you might you are not very successful at this. You may do this so quickly in fact that you don't even know how you felt. You may appear to be a thinking type person but you really are not. This is only a cover-up job.

Here your fifth chakra is rushing to take over from any fourth chakra expression. However it is so focused on controlling emotion that it functions in a limited manner only. Your third chakra tends to be underused and you often fail to act or move in lieu of all this attempt to figure out your feelings.

Healing.

You need to learn that your emotional reaction to things is just fine and needs no explanation to anyone including yourself. Allow your intellect to do more appropriate activities like figuring out crossword puzzles or plotting a route for your vacation. That is what it is for, not to be constantly on your tail. This will develop your fifth chakra in a well rounded way and take the pressure off your fourth chakra so that it can blossom.

Again, you need to do physical labor or engage in sports where you get regular physical workouts and get your energy moving. You need to develop that third chakra so that you can take action right when you need to. Meditations and concentrations on that chakra will be helpful. You will find that when you act, you will tend to move away from your trap and move toward healing.

Emotional center first-----moving trap.

Imbalance

You are a feeling type person quick to experience emotion. You have an affinity for art and music and you are naturally perceptive and intuitive. However, as before, when you are stressed you have trouble accepting your feelings and quickly rush to do something about them. So, you become trapped in impulsive action that tends to shut off your feelings. You tend to do this with no intellectual input. You can become extremely impulsive and act out in a variety of destructive ways. If someone hurts your feelings you are likely to lash out at them or run off and go on a shopping spree to make yourself feel better.

When you react like this you are neither feeling your emotions adequately nor are you truly acting efficiently or productively.

Here, your fourth chakra is held hostage by your third chakra while your fifth chakra has no say in the matter because it is shut down. Whatever grief you are holding in your fourth chakra dictates avoidant behavior from your third chakra and cuts down on your natural and healthy expression of feelings.

Healing

As a naturally emotional person you are intuitive and perceptive. However you need to eliminate the habit of cutting off the feeling by impulsively acting out. This means having the courage to face your emotions by letting them be and express themselves. When you are sad, be sad. When you are angry, say what you are angry about instead of driving recklessly or bashing someone. Your moving center needs to be directed to more appropriate activity such as sports and hard physical work. Your intellectual center needs to be moved forward into more activity. Read philosophy; play chess or bridge; study a language; engage in writing or public speaking to develop word usage.

Moving center first-----intellectual trap

Imbalance

Basically you are an action oriented person, highly co-ordinated and gifted in the knowledge of how to use your body. However when your intellectual trap comes into play, usually under stress, you stop the action to think about it instead. Thus your fine sense of timing is interrupted and you lose the rhythm of your natural response. For example, imagine what happens when you stop to think about your feet when you are involved in a complex dance routine. Imagine a drummer stopping to think about which drum to strike with what hand during a performance. The natural flow is blocked and the result is disconnection. You become imbalanced and trapped when intellect cuts off the action out of habit.

Here the natural flow of activity from your third chakra is cut off by the fifth chakra, the word center. For example. "Let's see, was that the right hand or the left hand first, no, maybe it is the right leg first." and so on.

Notice that emotions are left out in this process and it is the reason why many engineers are accused of having no sensitivity. They are often experts at thinking through the steps and movements of machines and so on. Yet they often forget about the aesthetics. Likewise, people who are trapped here tend to engage in endless planning and rehearsing rather than actually experiencing the event or relationship. This is where the emotion lies, in the event itself, not in the planning. Making love is an emotional experience. Planning to make love is more calculated.

Healing

Since you are naturally action oriented, you need to trust these impulses more immediately. Allow the body to move, let the natural rhythms take over. This is not to say you should never think. Thinking can be useful if you are deliberately using your intellectual center to choreograph a dance or program some machinery, that is, thinking through the steps in advance. However when you are finished planning, it is time to let intellectual center go and return to the more spontaneous movements of your body. Allow yourself to experience an entire day without planning anything. Just let things unfold. Emotions need to be cultivated through allowing yourself to actually experience the event that you keep at bay through your constant planning. Surrendering to intimacy is a great healer here.

Moving center first----emotional trap

Imbalance

At first impulse you are also naturally action oriented. You too, have the co-ordination and natural rhythm of all moving centered people. However under stress, you allow your emotions to interrupt your natural flow and this traps you into some very negative habit patterns. For example you can become addicted easily to gambling or substance abuse because of the knee jerk reaction of action and emotion with no intellectual center input.

You down a drink and you like the way you feel so you down another one and on and on. You pull the slot machine lever and get an emotional thrill when the coins spill out. This prompts more action leading to the thrill of more pseudo emotion. Your intellectual center is shut off so that you can't hear it tell you that your actions are destructive and will have negative consequences, such as your losing all your money.

Here, your well developed third chakra is constantly interfered with by the pain in your fourth chakra. You have chosen to become compulsive instead. The third chakra is held hostage by the need for the fourth chakra to be shut down.

Healing

You need healthy outlets for the natural action of your body. Sports and travel and anything action oriented can be the source of tremendous satisfaction if it is not overly linked with stress. Many excellent athletes destroy their careers when the sport they love becomes overly competitive and therefore stressful. Return the activity to the level of fun and you return to a state of balance.

Introduce yourself to the active use of your intellectual center. Read some philosophy. Engage in more planning. Do your own accounting. Take a public speaking class and develop your use of language. Develop your fifth chakra. Open the fourth chakra and allow the pain and the grief to release appropriately rather than act it out through wild or self destructive actions.

Develop the ability to think and allow this thoughtful verbal expression to balance your actions and your feelings.

Chapter Ten

The Instinctive Center

The instinctive or survival oriented center has more influence on imbalance and healing than you might ever imagine. Within the instinctive center is stored all urges to eat, all urges to breathe, procreate, sleep, squint and sneeze from dust, and an endless array of behaviors that you take for granted or give little thought to unless disturbed in some way. When these become disturbed or act out of balance, the instinctive center requires processing and healing.

The neutral instinctive center is the hub of the wheel, so to speak, for all your other center's activities. All centers are linked to the instinctive center and act in coordination with it. Thus we can not speak about healing without a thorough discussion of how your instinctive center works.

You have learned that you need your intellectual center to solve problems that help you survive. Therefore all useful intellectual thoughts have been stored in your instinctive center if they at one time helped you to survive. The same is true for the feelings of emotional center and the actions of moving center. You have learned that love, anger, humor etc are all conducive to surviving. You have also learned that to run, climb, crawl and so on are likewise conducive to survival at certain times. Your instinctive center stores and rearranges all the information neatly each lifetime in a way that serves you the best.

Your life plan, consisting of your overleaves, life task, self-karma, and astrological make up, determines how the information is stored in the instinctive center. In addition, the karma you have targeted to complete this lifetime determines the accessibility of information stored there. We will discuss this in greater detail shortly.

Although the instinctive center governs your first chakra, the survival chakra, this center has connections to all seven chakras. Think of your instinctive center then as a library, memory bank, or storehouse of all memories from all lifetimes about any information that can contribute to your survival. Often called the subconscious mind by psychologists, it can be accessed deliberately by creating a relaxed and altered state. The instinctive center can then be explored and reorganized consciously.

HOW THE INSTINCTIVE CENTER IS STRUCTURED

Think of the instinctive center as a ball with layers as you might see in an onion. The layers near the surface are the ones most readily accessible. The deeper or core layers are not so available and are more difficult to access.

The instinctive center has two main tiers of survival information. These tiers can be subdivided into many layers as well.

The Core.

The core of the instinctive center is made up of permanently stored past life information. Think of this core as being deeply buried under many layers. The actual source of the problem is then less visible. This core also has several layers of accessibility. The first layer is made up of information that was stored based on trauma in a past life but is very unlikely to happen again.

> *For example you may have had the unlikely experience of being struck by a meteor in a past life and it maimed you. Since it is a highly unusual event, it is not readily remembered nor does it push for recognition in a later life.   It is the most deeply buried level of information.*

The second layer of the core is made up of traumatic experiences that have occurred a number of times in various lifetimes and therefore are much more reactivating in general. However this information is not likely to be used in your current lifetime if your life circumstances don't bring it up.

> *For example you may have drowned on a number of occasions in past lives, so you have fears about being on large bodies of water. But since that is not the lesson you wish to work on this lifetime, you have chosen to be born and raised in the desert. The instinctive center fears are therefore latent.*

The third layer of the core has to do with information based on past life experiences that is relevant to the experiences that you are having in this lifetime. So that if you choose to live by the sea, all the lives when you drowned are neatly arranged or filed for immediate accessibility.

Now, it is important to realize that your instinctive center is not only a storehouse of threatening information but that it includes all useful tidbits that contribute toward survival. Thus it has stored, for example the fact that fresh air and drinking water contribute to longevity as well as rest and relaxation. Since these are rarely recorded with the kind of intensity that the traumas are, they are not as likely to push for recognition with the same amount of urgency. Likewise some of this information is not as pertinent to this lifetime as other memories are.

This is why it is so easy for people to ignore the need for fresh air or uncontaminated food and water. Eventually, as environmental conditions worsen, these memories will begin to push for greater recognition. This has already begun for many of the older souls.

The Surface Level

The topmost or surface layers of information have to do with survival information stored this lifetime through your cultural and familial imprinting, and from direct threats and trauma to your body. Think of this level as being the most accessible to your conscious awareness.

This level of your instinctive center has several layers. The first two layers have to do with survival information that is second hand. The first layer has to do with fears that you adopt directly from your main imprinters.

> *Thus if your mother has an inordinate fear of red cars, even though you have had no past life or present experiences with red cars, you can have a panic reaction to them. This kind of imprinting can be tough to shake at first, but will readily drop away when you can see the source of your fear. You discover that the fear is not truly your own. Upon insight you say, "Oh, that's Dad's fear, or Mom's fear, not mine."*

The second layer is survival information that you pick up from secondary imprinters like your cultural or societal groups.

So, for example if you are taught by your society to fear black people or white people even though you have had no experiences with them, you will tend to have fears when you first make contact with them. This type of fear is easier to shake when you have positive initial experiences with people from the feared group or race. Infant and baby souls who rely on secondary imprinting primarily will have a more difficult time letting go of their learned reactions.

The third layer of this surface level is survival information that you have stored based on your own personal experience.

If you were beaten repeatedly by your father, uncles, and brothers, your fear of men is based on your direct experience. This level of instinctive fear can be tenacious and is the kind of information that is so intense that you store it permanently for other lifetimes. This stored information, as you will see, forms the second tier of the instinctive center.

The fourth layer of the surface level of instinctive information is made up of associations derived from the third layer.

So for example if you were beaten by your uncles etc., and they always wore blue shirts, then every time you see a blue shirt, you will tend to get instinctive center reactivation. These associations can sometimes get rather divorced from the original event or experience and can look like a phobia, an irrational fear. With a little guidance it can usually be traced to its source this lifetime and released.

To accomplish this, focus on the feared object, sense the part of your body that reacts and refocus on this spot or area. As you do so, watch the mental images or memories that come to mind. They may be mere snatches or feelings rather than clear pictures. These feelings, senses, or pictures will lead you directly toward the original source of the fear. Release comes with recognition of the original event and the expression of that emotion. We will discuss this more thoroughly shortly.

THE STRUCTURE OF THE INSTINCTIVE CENTER

MOVING PART

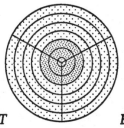

INTELLECTUAL PART   *EMOTIONAL PART*

layer 4. association to direct experience.
layer 3. direct personal experience.
layer 2. cultural imprinted information
layer 1. familial imprinted information.

SURFACE LEVEL: **Present life information.**

layer 3. events related to this life
layer 2. events not highly relevant to this life.
layer 1. unusual circumstances; not relevant.

CORE: **Past life information.**

Both the core and the surface level have three main sections each, one section for each of the three centers, emotional, intellectual, and moving.

1. The moving part of the instinctive center stores all the information you need to keep your body functioning and in constant repair. In other words it governs your autonomic nervous system, heart rate, blood pressure, digestion, metabolism, etc. This section stores accumulated knowledge that is relevant to keeping your body safe. If you have frozen to death on a number of occasions, then you will have an aversion to cold and so on.

2. The emotional part of the instinctive center stores all karmic debts and ribbons from past lives. These are stored according to intensity or impact on you and relevance to the present life. Thus the knowledge of having been abandoned by someone in a past life is stored here as well as the intensity of emotion that it caused you.

    The intensity of self karmic lessons that you have chosen this lifetime is stored here as well. Often this represents a theme that you have been working on over a set of lifetimes. For example, you may have been careless and self destructive with your physical body on a number of occasions. You can be working on having more compassion for your physical body and learning to treat it with respect and care.

3. The intellectual part of the instinctive center acts as a clearing house, deciding which information is relevant to the present situation and which is not. It

works largely by association and is subconscious in nature. That is, you are mostly not aware of its processing. You can learn to be more conscious of its operations through attention and focus. This is the part that you can interact with and speak with during concentration or self hypnosis.

HOW YOUR INSTINCTIVE CENTER WORKS.

Your instinctive center works very much like the way a computer operates. It can store a vast amount of information and arrange it in an infinite variety of ways. It's retrieval properties are awesome and it can perform an complex set of operations in a twinkling of an eye. Yet it is not particularly intelligent. It functions on a black-white, yes-no model of operation. It does not see shades of grey. It merely scans the environment and delivers up any information that might be relevant to the immediate experience. This is the activity of the intellectual part of the instinctive center.

You may be asked to undergo superficial surgery to remove a foreign matter like a splinter and have an exaggerated fear response that keeps you from undergoing this beneficial treatment. Your instinctive reaction to the surgical knife is based on several past life associations wherein you died in surgery. Your instinctive center does not distinguish between the benevolence of the surgery now and the deadly nature of the surgery then. What is needed here is the conscious recognition of the nature and source of the fear. Along with this recognition, the intensity of the fear must be released and the memories refiled for later use.

The instinctive center then becomes catalyzed whenever you experience an actual or a perceived threat. If a bear approaches you in the forest your instinctive center instantly records the event (emotional part) and matches it (intellectual part) with any information that it has about the nature of bears in your experience either from your imprinting this lifetime, your associations to bearness, and from any past life experiences with bears. If it judges that the bear is a threat, you will receive an instantaneous rush of adrenalin that encourages you to flee to safety (moving part). This happens before your conscious self has time to operate and figure out what kind of bear this is. Nor will you have the opportunity to be aesthetically pleased by the bears coloration or graceful stride as it shortens the distance between you and it.   However, you may suddenly perceive that the bear is really just a log that in the dim light of the forest just looked like a bear.   In this case the intellectual part of the instinctive center over-rides the moving part and the emotional part and you calm down.

Your instinctive center stores information by association. This is true within each layer and between layers. If you were to visually see the lines of association, what you would see would be ribbons or strings of connections, each one leading to another. These strings of association branch out within the layer and form a ribbon between layers. This is what we mean when we say karmic ribbon. You have ribbons of similar thoughts, feelings, and actions related to intense recorded experiences, this lifetime and other lifetimes. When you have a self-karmic ribbon, you have a string of experiences that are related to personal lessons. When you have a karmic ribbon, you have an associated string of events that relate to another person.   In either case, what keeps them an active ribbon, is their unfinished and therefore imbalanced nature.

When you discover balance, learn the lesson, complete the business, these events are no longer stored by association but relegated to storage files in your instinctive center. They become available for reference but do not necessarily push upward for recognition.

The more business you complete, the more energy you release from holding ribbons together. That is why, when you complete a karma, you feel such a release.   You can imagine the kind of energy available to a late level old soul or transcendental soul who has resolved the majority of their karma.

HOW TO WORK WITH YOUR INSTINCTIVE CENTER

Knowing that your instinctive center works efficiently with a low IQ, is a key to getting into harmony with it. When you understand how to communicate with and work with your instinctive center, you have a handle on one of the most powerful self healing tools you possess.

The first thing to realize is that although your instinctive center can cause you difficulty, it is dedicated to preserving your physical body at all costs. This is its primary function. Your body needs to live long enough so that you can experience the kinds of lessons and challenges that the Earth has to offer. Therefore it is performing a noble function.

The second thing to realize is that your instinctive center is not highly intellectual nor is it devious. It merely does what it is programmed to do. It can be directly communicated with and will respond to specific instructions. It operates specifically according to the laws described above. It functions at the rational level of a small child.   If it clearly understands that there is no immediate threat, it will relax its reactivation. If not, it will man or woman its post with hypervigilance for an infinite amount of time. Keep in mind that this has nothing to do with how intelligent or intellectual you are. A very intelligent person acts deviously but primitively when the instinctive center is out of balance. You can readily see this in any person who is actively paranoid.

The third thing to understand is that your imagination is the primary channel of communication between you and your instinctive center. For example, all you have to do is imagine a giant threatening spider crawling up your leg or a beady eyed cobra dancing and ready to strike you and you will have a physiological response that tells you your instinctive center has been re-activated.

In the same way you can use your imagination to calm your instinctive center and trace its associations back to the source of the problem.

Your instinctive center memories that are relevant for this lifetime, are stored by association in the cells of your body parts. A method for accessing this information was described in the book "Tao to Earth" under the section "Storing Imprinting in the Body". Because this is such a valuable method for working with your instinctive center we will repeat some of that information here. We are going under the assumption that you cannot hear about this method too many times, from different vantage points.

1. Begin by parking your body in a comfortable and relaxed place. Allow yourself to go into a mild trance state by focusing on your outbreath six or seven times. Select a focus that you wish to work on. Perhaps you have an irrational fear of the dark and you want to get to the bottom of this fear.

2. In order to trace the instinctive center memories you will need to focus on the part of your body that has the strongest sensation when you imagine the situation that reactivates you. Your instinctive center will automatically reactivate the body part connected with your fear or problem.

Imagine walking alone into a dark room, building, cave, or forest, whatever is most frightening to you. Notice the sensations that this produces in your body. For example you might feel a pressure in your solar plexus or a sharp pain under your lower right ribs.

3. Focus on this area in your body and describe it to yourself as best you can. Perhaps it feels like a sharp hot needle between your two middle ribs just under your right nipple. Maybe it feels like it would look dark purple and there is a kind of terror about it.

4. Allow your imagination to create pictures in your minds eye. Because you are focusing on a specific body part, your imagination will automatically call forth pictures from your instinctive center that are directly related to that body part.

5. Be willing to accept whatever pictures and emotions come up for review. You may experience yourself in a dark forest with a dark shape looming up on your right. Stick with the images and see where they lead you. There may be an image of ragged looking assassin with stinking breath stabbing a sharp knife between your ribs as you gasp and stumble with shock and surprise. Stick with the images and carry them through even until after you experience dying. Ask yourself, "What did I learn? What did I hold onto? What happened there? What was that all about. Who was that? Do I know them now?" and so on and so forth until you are completely satisfied.

6. If you wish, you might like to replay the event with several different outcomes. For example perhaps you disarm your assailant and chase him off, leading you to live a long, satisfying and productive life.

7. Check in on the body part that you started with. Is it still in pain or discomfort. If so repeat the last two steps going over each new set of images to completion. You may have to do this a number of times until all the pain and tension has been released.

If you do feel a release emotionally and physically, focus on your fear of the dark again. If it does not produce any physical sensations you are balanced again. If you do get a different physical sensation, then repeat steps three onward again. It is not unusual to have several rounds at this, especially if you have had a lot of lifetimes.

Breathing

You may wish to begin the process by deepening your breathing. Note that this tends to intensify the experience and can allow you to reach deeper levels of the instinctive center. When the breathing is coupled with the gradual build up of appropriate music, the experience can be profound.   It is recommended that you not do this alone but request the support of a competent guide or helper.

Deep and rapid breathing, with the intention of working with unresolved personal dynamics, can produce a variety of responses. First it will tend to focus you more on the part of your body that has stored instinctive center memories.   As the discomfort increases in that part of your body, you can actually have a competent bodyworker help you to discharge and release the stress held there.   This can have powerful therapeutic effects.

Secondly, the breathing can intensify the associated memories, and thereby increase the emotional release that you experience as they surface. If you resist or fight them however, your pain can intensify unbearably. Therefore, if you are not willing to feel or see what is there, you would do better to avoid this technique.

Thirdly, the breathing helps to get to the source of the unfinished business. As you follow the trail to its origination, you may experience a kind of regression. If the source has to do with decisions that you made about this lifetime, based on lessons you wanted to learn, then you will probably experience a kind of regression back to birth and pre-birth memories. You may actually re-live the intensity of birth, and recall the thoughts and feelings you had, as you delivered yourself into the karma of this life.

There are several important thoughts to hold while proceeding with this technique. One is to remember that all is chosen by you. All the memories are based on choices you have made to experience and play the earth game. Avoid the temptation to judge the choices. Observe and accept whatever surfaces. All the instinctive memories are related to survival of some kind. Remember that your instinctive center is designed to keep you alive. Therefore, even if you recall a past life suicide, in a distorted way, the action was taken based on information that led you to believe that this was better than pain. The memory is kept to help you survive better in the future.

To do this all at one sitting may be overwhelming so you might need to spread out the review over a period of days or weeks. It is also helpful to have a guide, counselor, or friend with you to help you go through the entire process.

As your instinctive center throws up the memories either actually or symbolically, you re-experience them and the emotional intensity that recorded them. In this way your emotional center becomes balanced. You also ask a series of questions to balance the need for your intellectual center to know.

You run through other possible scenarios to balance your moving center. In the end you have processed yourself out of a state of imbalance. You have consciously worked with your instinctive center and re-organized the information it carries about your survival. You have relegated its records about dark places to back files. Now you are more free to function appropriately.

SELF KARMA, KARMA AND THE INSTINCTIVE CENTER.

As we mentioned earlier, your instinctive center is a repository for incomplete karmic ribbons and self karmic lessons. It is that part of you that keeps the balance sheets as well as translates essence level satisfaction over lessons learned. If essence is not completely satisfied that a lesson has been learned, your instinctive center will be the first to know it. Therefore, you can often know what your karma or self karma is, by consulting with or paying attention to your instinctive center.

Should you have an intense fear reaction to a situation or event, you may be sure that you have lessons to learn in that area. For example, if you are intensely afraid of crowded places, you have a self karma that involves safety with other people. Essence will never be satisfied until that fear is cleared or reduced to neutrality. In some ways, that fear is like an open wound calling out for attention and healing. One way you can handle the fear is of course by avoiding crowds altogether and sparing yourself the discomfort of the experience. You may do this for several lifetimes but you have not healed the event. You are handicapped by your fear of crowded places. Healing results from facing the fear directly, experiencing the emotional value of it, and telling the truth about the whole experience to yourself. When this happens, essence is satisfied that the lesson was learned or the experience was completed. The instinctive center no longer reacts to crowds.

Facing the fear means recognizing that you have the fear in the first place and having the desire or intention to work with it. You do not have to know how you will do this. In fact, at this stage you may feel that your fear is insurmountable and overwhelming. Your false personality usually feels this way. It is not able to solve any problems by itself. The trick is to get false personality under control enough, and quiet enough for essence to lend its support. When you have opened up a line of communication with essence, the problem or fear begins to fall apart, no matter how big the obstacle.

Your desire to face the fear opens up that line of communication with essence via the instinctive center.

Experiencing the emotional value of the experience means being willing to stay present enough to feel the sensations and intensity served up by the instinctive center without avoidance. The services of a trained helper may be necessary at this point but ultimately this must be personally experienced.

Telling the truth about the whole experience means recognizing the lesson or meaning of the event. This is the "aha" of the big picture perspective that happens only after the emotion has been faced. So, you may say, "Aha, now I see that my fear of crowds has to do with my fear that I will die if I let people get physically close to me." If you want to know what needs healing, then ask yourself, "What am I afraid of?"

Instinctive review

Approximately every twenty five years in a given lifetime, you automatically experience a major instinctive center review. Every twelve years you go through a minor review. This is a built in structure that helps you to periodically review, file, and complete processing your accumulated experiences thus far. This is not a highly conscious event but it is noticeable in several ways. During these periods of review, you are likely to experience a kind of slowing down of external events as you concentrate on your inner life. You may need to sleep more, be solitary, and feel your emotions to a greater extent. If you resist this natural process you will tend to experience a great deal of frustration because you will not be able to get a lot done externally. Nevertheless, typically people resist these times resulting in an accumulation of unfinished business over lifetimes.

These periodic reviews are wonderful opportunities to transform blocks, imbalances, and obstacles accumulated over time. Because the instinctive center is more accessible during the review, it is more amenable to direct intervention and balancing. Counseling, hypnosis, concentration, meditation, energy work, and body work are more productive and produce better results during the review. Personal retreats, vision quests, and spiritual practices are quite helpful. You can evolve into your next level of growth, leaving the baggage behind.

An excellent practice in this time of review, is the examination of parallel lives for creative spark and inspiration. This is a way of checking out your options and choices. Parallel lives are those possibilities that you have not been focusing on in this physical existence, but you are nonetheless living out in other parallel time frames. By visualizing and concentrating, you can touch into these parallels to see what you have actualized had you made other choices. If you like what you see you can re-intercept those parallels through an act of choice. For a full discussion see the section on parallel universes in "Tao to Earth".

Instinctive centered episodes and lifetimes

Should you regularly resist your opportunity for instinctive center review, you will gradually build a greater and greater need for balance in your so called future. When the pressure builds, due to lessons not completed, you may need to resort to desperate measures to regain balance. A temporary psychotic episode may fill the bill or, in the event of too much buildup, you will arrange for an instinctively centered lifetime. This usually looks like a lifetime of severe emotional disturbance or psychosis. This forces you to ignore everything else in your life but the unfinished business at hand. This is a vast topic and cannot be adequately described in this volume. It will be discussed in full in a volume about mental illness.

Chapter Eleven

Goals and Modes as Vehicles of Healing

GOALS

One excellent way to understand imbalance and the healing process is to study the positive and negative poles of your overleaves or personality traits. These will show you instantly, the actions, reactions, and attitudes that lead to disease or healing. Some of the overleaves such as goals, modes, and the traps of centers can lead to substantial imbalance if they are expressed negatively. Other overleaves such as attitudes and chief features can contribute to the imbalance of the goals, modes, and centers by skewing them one way or another.

Resistance to your life goal is the greatest source of disease that you can find. Not only do you resist your goals, but you often feel frustrated, because you have not yet learned how to reach them successfully. This too can be a source of disease or illness.

Remember that your goal is your primary motivator in life, that which you strive to achieve on an hour by hour, day by day basis. You choose your goal prior to birth in the physical form in order to give you a theme, a structure, a focus around which your main lessons revolve. This gives your lifetime a sense of order and focus.

Just because you have a particular goal does not necessarily mean that you do it well or act in the positive pole. For example if your goal is Dominance, you are always motivated to win or lead, however, you may not know how to do this appropriately in every situation. You may make many errors and attempt ineffective maneuvers that bring you face to face with the challenge of the task. That is why it is your chosen goal, to learn how to master it over the course of your life. You gradually learn how to operate from the positive pole.

The goal, as with all the overleaves, tends to slide, on occasion, to the polar goal on the axis. If your goal is Acceptance, you will tend to slide momentarily to Discrimination and vice-versa. If your goal is Relaxation, you will tend to slide to any goal as needed for the most convenience.

Here are the seven life goals shown in their axis.

GOAL:		AXIS:
Ordinal	Exalted	
DISCRIMINATION---ACCEPTANCE		Expression
SUBMISSION----------DOMINANCE		Action
RE-EVALUATION-------GROWTH		Inspiration
Neutral		
RELAXATION		Assimilation

Your goal will often determine how you become ill or in what arena your discomfort will arise. Likewise, the nature of your chosen goal will determine whether your imbalance is an intellectual, emotional, energetic, or instinctive one. Since your goal is what motivates you in life, it is what drives you to seek out specific experiences. The outcome of these experiences either frustrates your efforts or signals success in achieving your ultimate goal.   When your efforts are frustrated or when you resist the lesson you become imbalanced and experience the negative pole of your goal. The result is usually illness in one of the three spheres. On the other hand when you operate out of the positive pole of your goal you not only heal yourself but you heal everyone around you.

Here is how each goal tends to affect you when you experience it in the negative pole. Here also is how you can heal the imbalance.

+sophistication

DISCRIMINATION: Emotional imbalance. Emotional healing.
The fifth chakra.

-rejection

Imbalance:

The negative pole of the goal of discrimination is rejection, an action and a reaction that amplifies an emotional imbalance. The act of rejecting and the feeling of being rejected are intensely emotional, and tend to foster more frustrating emotions. When you set up a situation where you are chronically rejected, such as being with a mate who does not love you, you are creating a condition of emotional imbalance. You are focusing your attention on the negative quality of rejection.

Likewise when you spend your time rejecting every person and every situation, you are expressing only a part of the discriminatory energies of the fifth chakra.   You create an imbalance here that can result in intense emotional outbreaks.

Healing:

On the other hand, the positive pole of discrimination, sophistication, heals emotional imbalance by making rejection serve a higher purpose. When you select out only a few good friends to be with, your attention is drawn to the pleasure of these friendships rather than to the others that you cut off.

When you are discriminating, you feel good and you express good judgement. For you, this is the healing path.

+ agape

ACCEPTANCE: Emotional and physical imbalance. Emotional
and physical healing. The fourth chakra.

-ingratiation

Imbalance:

The negative pole of acceptance is ingratiation, an experience that causes an increase in feeling and emotionality. Ingratiation, doing or saying anything to be liked, is a result of the fear of non-acceptance. So, as you can see, ingratiation is an emotional experience all the way around. The wish for acceptance can be so strong that emotional stress results in a physical problem as well. Becoming ill is a well known vehicle for sympathy and attention. Both forms of imbalance are a result of the passive expression of this goal. That is, they have to do with the hope for acceptance rather than the active initiation of it.

Ingratiation can result, in part, from a closed off fourth chakra. When you are out of affinity with yourself, or in a state of non-acceptance, you fear that you will not be accepted by others either. You tend to ingratiate and further shut down your heart chakra. Physically this can manifest as heart disease, asthma, and other cardiovascular disorders. Emotionally the reaction is depression or anxiety.

Healing:

Agape or unconditional acceptance are the natural antidote for the emotional and physical imbalance resulting from ingratiation. To actively accept your situation or unconditionally accept another is to put yourself in the drivers seat. You relax and let go as you open up to others. To unconditionally accept yourself, is the ultimate healing.

Always look to see whether you are accepting yourself before making efforts to accept others. Agape is a form of expression. Is your expression making you feel good? If so, you are on the path to healing.

+ evolution

GROWTH: Physical imbalance. Physical healing. The sixth chakra.

-confusion

Imbalance:

The negative pole of growth is confusion. Confusion occurs when you exert too much effort and you cannot tolerate any more growth. You overwhelm your capacity to understand and process your experience and you feel the unpleasantness of overload. For example, you might enter into three new intense relationships at the same time, thinking that you can only grow from this, and the result is overwhelm, with no evolution at all. Likewise you may feel the urge to try four different types of meditation that you learned this week, only to end up entirely confused. Evolution comes to a halt.

The sixth chakra is related to the goal of growth because it is here that you try to understand your evolution and development. When the sixth chakra shuts down or becomes overworked you experience confusion and sometimes headaches.

Sometimes you attempt to grow by barking up the wrong tree. For example you might feel that taking a little L.S.D. will help you to evolve. Whereas once this might have worked for you, this time you feel overwhelmed and the result is massive confusion. Confusion has a way of running you down physically and the result is imbalance on a physical level. Therefore people with a goal of growth usually become physically ill more often than those with other goals.

Healing:

Healing results when you arrive at the positive pole, evolution, and you integrate growth at a natural pace. You use your sixth chakra to perceive each step in your growth process and you experience breakthroughs and ah-ha's rather than confusion. Your body is more relaxed and able to handle the natural tension in the growth curve. You can remain physically healthy because you are no longer driving yourself beyond your limits.

You know you are evolving when you feel energized and physically healthy. Find a pace that works for you and avoid overload. Evolution is inspiring. Do you feel inspired?

+ simplicity

RE-EVALUATION: Energetic imbalance. Energetic healing. The first chakra.

-withdrawal

Imbalance:

The negative pole of re-evaluation is withdrawal. Withdrawal takes place when you make life so complicated and strained that you cannot face anyone anymore and you retreat into hibernation. This is especially common for people with disabilities who, rather than making the best of what they can do in a relatively simple fashion, resist their situation and withdraw or deny that anything is wrong. Their first chakra can shut down to such a degree that they are barely surviving.

Likewise people who fight the single main theme that their life is about, like for example a prisoner with a life sentence, can withdraw from their life's potential and sulk for years. The result is an energetic imbalance where all the chakras are chronically underused. Apathy and listlessness can set in, further undermining the meaning and value of life.

Healing:

Simplicity in living is the cure for such an imbalance. The first chakra is operating at an even pace that does not so outstrip the higher chakras that they become paralyzed. Think of the simplicity in the life of the Birdman of Alcatraz, hardly a wasted life. His life was completely molded by two themes, life imprisonment and the care of birds.

Find the simplicity in tasks and in your way of life. When things become too complicated you are on the wrong track. When you find yourself simply smiling, then you are on the path of inspiration and healing.

+ devotion

SUBMISSION: Energetic imbalance. Energetic healing. The second chakra.

-subservience

Imbalance:

The negative pole of submission is subservience [exploited], the passive act of allowing another to control you. This results in cutting off the natural activity of your chakras, namely your third, fourth and fifth chakras. You tend to cut off your power, your self esteem, and your ability to communicate. To allow others to take advantage of you, is to give up your space energetically and create a massive imbalance in your energy flow.

On the other hand you tend to leave the second chakra too vulnerable to control by others. You allow yourself to be taken advantage of, and in a manner of speaking to leave yourself open to be raped in a metaphorical sense.

Healing:

Devotion heals this energetic imbalance by activating all the chakras and intending to use them in service of your chosen cause. Here you harness your power and open your self expression so that you can better devote yourself fully. Your devotion to your mate, family, job, or guru can be immensely healing not only for yourself but for those around you.

Learn to do things that bring out the devoted quality in you. A devoted person actively promotes another person, a belief system, or a cause. When you are doing this you are headed in a healing direction.

+leadership

DOMINANCE: Energetic imbalance. Energetic healing. The third chakra.

-dominance

Imbalance:

Dictatorship is the negative pole of the goal of dominance. When you attempt to control others and eliminate their freedom of choice, you   create an energetic imbalance in yourself. Typically in this type of imbalance the third chakra is used without the counter-balancing of the sixth chakra [perception and intuition] and the sensitivity of the fourth chakra [affinity]. When you act the dictator toward others, you automatically and unconsciously push yourself around as well. You try to control and force yourself to be or act a certain way. This tends to set up an internal rebellion that pits you against yourself.

Healing:

The healing for dictatorship is leadership, the act of serving others through assertiveness and responsible guidance. This tempers the power of the third chakra by allowing loving energy to flow from the fourth chakra and allow insight to issue from the sixth. This then makes you a powerful leader, one who not only leads with a desire for all to win but one who also loves yourself. A successful leader is one who can truly heal others energetically.

Find a way to win that includes what the other person wants as well. When you lead well, others will automatically follow. Look for this as a clue to your appropriate actions.

+ free-flowing

RELAXATION: Energetic, emotional, and physical imbalance.
    The ability to heal in all three spheres. The sixth chakra.

-inertia

Imbalance:

The negative pole of the goal of relaxation is inertia, a stuck, deadened place, where the enjoyment of living is on hold. This experience tends to cut off all the chakras, especially the sixth chakra, and the result can be depression followed by physical illness. Inertia also tends to affect other people by dulling their senses and cutting off the energetic flow and balance in their chakras as well. The result is that you feel and generate apathy.

Healing:

The healing quality of the goal of stagnation is flow, the effortless enjoyment of the natural process and course of life. When you operate out of the positive pole, flow, you can be enormously healing, energetically, emotionally, and physically to yourself as well as others. Your sixth chakra perception is open and helping you to see exactly what needs to be done from a state of effortlessness. In fact you function much more from a being aware state than a doing state.

Find the effortlessness in your tasks and in your daily affairs. If something is not working out, do not force it. It is probably not right for you. Your life can be easy if you let it.

MODES

Next to goals, modes can produce the most imbalance if expressed negatively. Since they are the method through which you operate and carry out all your activities, they have a substantial effect on you when you act from the negative pole. Since modes are more visible than goals are, it is often easier to see how you can get into trouble when you express them negatively.

As with goals, we will run through them and explain how they affect you in both a disease producing way and a healing way. Like goals they tend to affect different chakras and different levels of your consciousness.

Recall that your mode is your primary method, chosen prior to birth, for this lifetime of learning and experience. Your early parental and societal conditioning will determine aspects of your mode, but not the mode itself. Remember also, that there is a sliding action that takes you to your polar mode on the same axis. For example, if your mode is power, you will on occasion act cautiously or vice-versa. If you are in the neutral mode of observation, you will slide to any mode that you observe would be appropriate.

As with goals, you do not necessarily use your mode well at first. You may spend some time in the negative pole before you learn how to operate out of the positive pole more often.

Here are the seven modes:

MODES		AXIS
Ordinal	**Exalted**	
CAUTION------------------POWER		Expression
PERSEVERANCE--------AGGRESSION		Action
RESERVE------------------PASSION		Inspiration
Neutral		
OBSERVATION		Assimilation

+ deliberation

CAUTION: Emotional and energetic imbalance. Emotional and energetic healing. The first chakra.

-phobia

Imbalance:

The negative pole of caution mode is phobia, a response based on great fear and the desire to avoid the imagined danger. When you act phobically, you are in a heightened state of survival consciousness. Your first chakra is overly active and your fourth and sixth chakras are shut down. This state of affairs is intensely emotional and can lead you to act quite irrationally. This is accompanied by states of extreme anxiety and anger when you are faced with your worst fears.

You can remain physically healthy however, because your body is energized and ready for flight. Over a long period of time of course it can have a wearing effect on you physically, often resulting in minor colds or more seriously, in ulcers, colitis, or high blood pressure.

Healing:

Deliberation or the act of being deliberate is the healing quality in caution mode. Here, with careful forethought, you proceed at a slow but comfortable pace that allows you to be relaxed and feel safe. Your first chakra acts in harmony with the other six chakras and you feel energetically balanced as well as emotionally secure. From this place you can have a healing effect on others, because you have shown them how to avoid the dangers and achieve success by careful planning. They too will feel safe and secure.

Being deliberate is an expression of mastery over fear. You will find the deliberate side of caution mode when you move through your fear and find that you have survived.

+ authority

POWER: Energetic and emotional imbalance. Energetic and emotional healing. The third chakra.

-oppression

Imbalance:

The negative pole of power mode is oppression, a burdensome effort to control self or others by squashing the perceived opposition.   Here you tend to use the third chakra inappropriately toward others and you actually shut it down when you oppress yourself. When you do this you automatically shut down your fourth chakra and so your whole system becomes imbalanced.

Of course, this tends to make yourself and others feel uncomfortable, and contributes to intensely emotional states of negativity. Under prolonged conditions this can eventually work its way down to a physical level of distress, disrupting digestion and increasing blood pressure.

Healing:

On the other hand, when you use the positive pole of power mode, authority, you open your fourth chakra and heal your third chakra. Your energy runs smoothly and you respond with appropriateness toward the situation you are in. If you must take charge and move quickly in a time of danger you are perfectly capable of doing so. Your calm presence of power presents a picture of balance and lets others know that the situation is handled. They can then relax their fears and concentrate on the task at hand.

Authority is expressed. When you express your power, even without words, you will find yourself moving toward healing. When you do not express your power you oppress yourself.

+ restraint

RESERVE: Energetic imbalance. Energetic healing. Fifth chakra.

-inhibition

Imbalance:

Inhibition is the imbalancing negative pole of reserve mode. Here you shut down the expressiveness of your fifth chakra causing a reverberating effect throughout all your remaining chakras. Your energetic flow is blocked and the result is that you cannot act either. This is paralleled by an accompanying blockage in your fourth chakra and you end up feeling negative about yourself. When you self deprecate you can become more inhibited than ever and thus you are involved in a kind of vicious cycle.

Healing:

The healing quality of the mode of reserve is restraint. Here you conserve your energy and use it as a precision instrument as would a surgeon, a figure skater, a good chauffeur, or a ballet dancer. This tendency to refine your speech, your movements, and your use of energy has a balancing effect on your chakras, especially the expressive fifth one in the throat. The result is efficiency and beauty of expression and movement that has a healing effect on others. When you watch ballet or figure skating you are being healed by the refinement and beauty of movement and music.

Check to see if you are feeling inspired. Inhibition does not feel inspired. You will find that restraint is what creates the inspiration you are looking for.

+ self-actualization

PASSION: Physical and emotional imbalance. Physical and emotional healing. The fourth chakra.

-identification

Imbalance:

The negative pole of passion mode is identification, a loss of space or boundary between you and something else. When you are identified, you feel the same emotions as those that you are watching or listening to. Soap operas, news stories, gossip, and a friend's woes can become so real to you that you become overwhelmed with emotion and your ability to function normally may be impaired. Here your fourth chakra is wide open and the discrimination of your fifth chakra is underused or not functioning. The second chakra tends to be wide open as well, and you become attached to whoever or whatever is the object of your passion. You expend your energy unproductively and in some cases only add to the existing problems. This is the source of jealousy.

Physically, chronic identification can result in heart trouble and forms of cancer, both passionate and prolific illnesses.

Healing:

The positive pole of passion mode is self-actualization, the ability to throw yourself fully into something so completely that you become one with it in a positive way. A skier, for example, can become so engrossed in a run down the mountain that the skis literally become an extension of the legs. However if the skier fell and broke a ski, they would not be so identified with the ski that their personality would fall apart also. The skier is self actualized by the experience, not by the ski itself. Here the fourth chakra is open but balanced by the discriminating fifth chakra and the dynamic second chakra.

Self-actualization is so healing that the experience can literally cure so-called uncureable diseases. This of course, is a major inspiration for others. Being identified will feel bad whereas being self-actualized will feel good. Ask yourself what you are attached to. If you are attached to a person or thing you are probably identified. If you simply want the experience, you are headed for self-actualization.

+ persistence

PERSEVERANCE: Emotional imbalance. emotional healing. Third chakra.

unchanging

Imbalance:

The negative pole of perseverance mode is unchanging, a stuck pattern of unproductive repetition. Here you fall into a method of doing, that limits your options and sustains negative emotional intensity for long periods of time. Whether you persist in a rotten marriage or get stuck in a drinking habit, your emotional life gets caught in a chronic state of imbalance. The energy available from your third chakra is funnelled into one unproductive line of action to the exclusion of all other options. This tends to produce irritation, annoyance, or hopeless feelings in those you deal with. Your fifth chakra ability to discriminate and your sixth chakra ability to perceive tends to get shut down leaving you with "effort without insight". Perseverance tends to keep you going no matter what, so that physical illnesses do not get in the way.

Healing:

Discipline or persistence is the healing positive pole of perseverance mode. When you are able to stick to appropriate lines of action, you dissolve the obstacles in your path through repeated attempts. You feel balanced and proud of your efforts when you achieve success. Your third chakra functions in balance with your insight and your discriminatory powers. You automatically know when you have run into a blind alley and you change course. Like a disciplined athlete, you have the wisdom to know when to step up your efforts and when to take a break for needed rest and relaxation.

If your efforts are not producing the results you want, you are probably on the wrong track. Here, ask your intuition to tell you whether to proceed or not. If you cannot do this for yourself, consult a perceptive friend, counselor, or a psychic who can help you to see the truth.

+ dynamism

AGGRESSION: Energetic imbalance. Energetic healing. The second chakra.

-belligerence

Imbalance:

The negative pole of aggression, belligerence, creates imbalance energetically by exaggerating aggressive energy and shutting off balancing sensitivity. Here the second chakra becomes overly active while the fourth chakra tends to get shut off. Sexual energy is channeled to destructive ends without regard for love or harmony. The power and energy of the third chakra gets funnelled downward into the more negative qualities of the second chakra.

This is a state that can be manifested politically through governmental domestic and foreign policies. When the stance of a nation or state becomes belligerent toward its own people or toward other nations, the result is an energetic imbalance of the entire society whether it is the perpetrator or the target.

Healing:

Dynamism is the healing positive pole of aggression mode. Through dynamic action, much that is productive and evolutionary issues forth. The dynamic energy of the second chakra, tempered by fourth chakra love and affinity, literally, is responsible for the creation of the family. Dynamic aggression balanced by the feminine energy is the productive force in the physical universe. Aggression, when used with care, can heal by creating a dynamic energy flow that vitalizes all the chakras. Spending time with someone who truly loves and understands you, can help you find the dynamism in your aggression.

+ clarity

OBSERVATION: Emotional imbalance. Emotional healing. The sixth chakra.

-surveillance

Imbalance:

The imbalancing negative pole of observation is surveillance, a focused down use of sixth chakra perception for very limited purposes. When you go into surveillance you are scrutinizing the environment for anything that might pose as an imagined danger. In a battlefield situation this behavior might keep you alive and has a true purpose. However when you constantly survey your friends for possible criticism or when you survey yourself for any signs of vulnerability you are clearly headed for emotional imbalance. You become stressed and paranoid and in extreme cases can lose touch with reality. This is a state of extreme fear.

Healing:

The healing quality of observation is clarity. Clarity is the result of using the sixth chakra appropriately for purposes of understanding and not in service of fear, a first chakra emotion. Through clarity and insight most problems dissolve and balance is restored to your emotional life. Clarity is often made possible by resorting to the counsel of a friend, spouse, or professional, who may be able to help you see things more realistically.

HEALING AND BALANCE THROUGH POSITIVE POLES

The key to sliding into the positive poles of the overleaves is twofold.   First, working on eliminating your chief feature is crucial, because it is this that operates on fear and causes you to block the communications of essence. The seven chief features, self-destruction, greed, martyrdom, impatience, self-deprecation, arrogance, and stubbornness, primarily affect your goals and attitudes. Your primary chief feature affects your goal and your secondary chief feature affects your attitude.

If you are mostly self-deprecating, you will have difficulty with the goal of acceptance. If secondarily you are stubborn, you will find it difficult to be practical if you have the pragmatist attitude.

Secondly, eliminating the trap of your centering and finding greater balance among your centers will powerfully effect the way you handle your goals and modes.   Your centering, intellectual, emotional, and moving pushes you to react in specific ways. When you react from one main center to the exclusion of the others, or when you react from the trap of your center, you are creating automatic imbalance.

PART FOUR

CONSOLIDATION

Chapter Twelve

A Quick Review

PUTTING IT ALL TOGETHER

In the preceding chapters you have read about the key steps involved in spiritual evolution. You have become acquainted with the tools to accelerate the expansion of your awareness and processes to open you to ever higher degrees of your essence. You have learned of planetary and spiritual helpers that offer support and guidance along your path. You have discovered the importance of balance, the actions that lead to imbalance, and the steps that lead to healing and transformation.

Here, in these final pages, we will review the basics about those steps and processes that lead you toward balance and enlightenment. We will show you how, within the context of your everyday life, you can shift from a slow inevitable bumbling growth to conscious, dynamic, joy filled evolution.

SPIRITUAL GROWTH

Remember that the spiritual person is an awake and conscious individual who is aware of essence, and evolving along a path of cooperation with essence plans. The spiritual person begins to manifest their true soul age and embarks on a journey that ultimately reminds them of their true nature, their source in the Tao. They take risks, raise questions, and look within for the answers to those questions. The spiritual person is not without fear, but learns to transform that terror into the excitement and challenge of discovery. Recall the seven aims of being more awake.

1. To act your soul age.

2. To disidentify.

3. To take risks.

4. To integrate personality and essence.

5. To remember the Tao.

6. To attain balance.

7. To be effective.

Ultimately, spirituality means following the trail of unconditional acceptance of self and others. It means discovering a sense of detachment and disidentification from things, events, and situations.   This does not mean giving up or becoming apathetic and despairing over the task of changing seemingly impossible conditions such as poverty, hunger, and physical disease. It means discovering a place of peace within, even in the most trying condition that you are attempting to work in. Recall the seven steps leading you to unconditional self acceptance.

1. Trust your perceptions.

2. Be ruthlessly truthful with yourself.

3. Develop tolerance and recognize the perfection of the Tao in all things.

4. Be powerful appropriately.

5. Erase fear and your chief negative feature.

6. Surrender to Essence. Let Essence lead.

7. Be humble.

The evolutionary spiritual path ultimately follows the route mapped out by the positive poles of your overleaves. The process of erasing the onus of the chief negative feature, the main perpetrator of negative pole activity, leads toward greater spiritual awareness. Notice that we did not say that you have to erase your chief feature to be spiritual. We said that you can realize great spiritual insight in the process of observing it and letting it go. In other words, you are spiritual when you are doing spiritual work. You do not have to be finished with it in your terms, to be spiritual. Spiritual work can look almost like anything. If in the act of creating karma you have a major insight into the Tao, you have been involved in spiritual work.

A man was about to murder a robber whom he had caught in the act of stealing game, the result of a successful rabbit hunt in a region stricken by drought. In a state of rage, he had struck down the man and was about to stab him when he realized that the man's life was worth more than a frugal meal. He managed to get his anger under control and instead shared a portion of the rabbit with the would-be thief. This man acted in a spiritual way because he listened to his essence. It was not what he was about to do that made a difference. It was what he did.

The experience of enlightenment is the experience of the higher centers. While the daily activity of your centers, intellectual, emotional, moving, and instinctive are necessary for your survival, it is the experience of your higher centers that reminds you of who you truly are. Therefore, the more higher centered experiences you have, the more enlightened you are. Enlightenment is a product of recognizing the Truth, Love, and Beauty experienced through the higher centers.

DEGREES OF ESSENCE

As you achieve greater balance by harmonizing the reactions of your centers, you begin to access the higher centers more. As you access the higher centers more often, you begin to experience a higher degree of enlightenment. As you experience greater enlightenment, you begin to recognize the degrees of essence that connect you to all seven planes within the Tao. And as you allow greater degrees of essence to penetrate within your body, you become increasingly effective at recognizing and cutting through the maya or illusion that masks the Tao. You begin to wake up.

TOOLS OF THE PLANET

You have learned that some of the ancient methods for achieving enlightenment worldwide, are still powerful tools for awakening. Meditation, Concentration, study, dancing, singing, chanting, fasting, and service are all highly effective methods for reaching the higher centers. Yet none of these powerful techniques guarantees essence communication. We know of fragments that practice none of these and are awakened beings. We know of many that practice them arduously, but who are so directed by the chief feature that they make little headway for all their efforts. The key to these practices then, is whether they act to reduce the chief feature.

Communicating with guides and helpers through channeling and meditation can be a powerful tool for the acceleration of your awareness. The knowledge of this teaching itself is brought to you via a channeled source. And yet, these teachings and guidance are no guarantee of spiritual awakening or acceleration. We know of many individuals who receive channeled information and use it to further the goals of false personality. Your intent and desire to allow essence direction, added to your discipline, determine the results you ultimately harvest.

Planetary tools offer an abundance of resources on your path to awakening. The elements including wind, fire, earth, and water are age old teachers and healers, reminding you of your source and your early experience with them in devic form. They speak with you and remind you gently or ruthlessly of the consequences of your actions.

Association with certain minerals, gemstones, and metals raise or lower the frequency of your body and assist you to handle your overleaves better. In addition they help you to tolerate and work with other peoples overleaves. When you wear them on your person or place them in your vicinity consciously, you increase their effectiveness and reap beneficial results. If because of the overleaves you have chosen, you are lacking in certain areas, you can use these rock helpers to provide you temporarily with the desired energy.

The contributions of the plant kingdom are obvious with their healing properties, dietary influences, and gifts of building materials and energy resources. The insect kingdom offers assistance with plant cultivation, food chain maintenance, and countless resources as yet untapped.

The animal kingdoms offer assistance in a variety of ways. They offer you the benefit of their companionship, labor, and natural products. Secondarily they provide you with archetypal guidance and instinctive wisdom in the art of survival. Your experience with them in devic form helped you to form who you are. Animals remind you of what you once knew but have chosen to forget. In live form and in metaphor they influence your use of overleaves, just as the mineral and plant kingdoms do.

THE POWER OF HEALING

We have spoken to you at length about the ways that you become imbalanced and how you choose this for lessons and growth. You have learned that all forms of imbalance and disease are inseparable from healing, they are literally two sides of the same coin. Likewise we have stated that all healing is ultimately self-healing, sourced in essence, and not false personality. Some states of imbalance are chosen for experience or for karma and are not healable until their time is due. Other states are healable in a twinkling as soon as you get the lesson.

You have also become acquainted with the process of disease that occurs in the four main areas of living. You experience these imbalances emotionally, intellectually, energetically, and physically following the patterns defined by the lower centers and the instinctive center.

Imbalances are deeply related to the thoughtforms that you let influence you at each step of your life. Healing too can come from the supportive thoughts of guides and others that you allow in. The more you give permission to the expression of your own thoughts and feelings, the more rapid the healing process.

We have mentioned key steps to the healing process that will rapidly assist you to balance imbalanced states.

1. Being present

2. Being grounded

3. Establishing an essence connection

4. Calling for support

5. Bringing in the higher planes for healing

6. Healing with your hands

7. Healing others

Everything on the planet has healing value. Plants, minerals, wind, water, temperature, earth, air, flowers, smells, power spots, colors, shapes all have healing properties when applied with consciousness and focus.

On the internal side, your dreams have powerful abilities to bring you back into balance on all levels. Imbalances from past lives and earlier this life are readily healed in the dream states when awareness is applied. Remembering dreams, interpreting, reflecting, interviewing, and redreaming are all ways you can use the power of your dreams for greater balance and harmony.

You have learned how the various soul ages respond to healing differently and how they each have their unique approaches to the healing arts. Likewise you have become acquainted with the ways that the roles respond to finding balance and healing and how they each approach the healing of others. With this knowledge you can more carefully choose your personal healer or practitioner and make better use of your own healing talents.

THE CHAKRAS

Knowledge of the Seven chakras and the many minor chakras is a key to correcting imbalances in the body and in the personality structure. Each chakra affects and is affected by the overleaves you have chosen for this lifetime. They are affected by your chief negative feature and negative pole activity in your overleaves. Knowing how they function, how they are layered, and how to work with them is a powerful advantage in learning how to self-heal.

The Seven Chakras

7. Crown

6. Brow

5. Throat

4. Heart

3. Solar Plexus

2. Abdominal

1. Root-base of spine.

These chakras are records of past and present life memories related to the specific activities they govern. If you are experienced as a soul, they hold much information and a considerable amount of unfinished business. If you are a very young soul, you will have little information to go on and therefore you will have to bumble along with your mistakes.

You have become familiar with the connections between the chakras and how they can become blocked due to traumatic or intense episodes. We have given you simple steps to unblock these connections and balance the overall energetic system. You have learned the power of light and color in working with the chakras and their connections.

CHAKRAS AND CENTERS

The centers, although generally related to each of the chakras, more accurately represent certain combinations of them. Their balance is intimately related to the balance and harmony of the chakras. Knowing how the centers work, and how you can get trapped in a center, helps greatly in understanding which chakras habitually become blocked or overused. With this knowledge you can directly intervene with your patterns of imbalance and learn to use your centers and your chakras efficiently and appropriately.

The seven centers

7. Higher Intellectual

6. Higher Emotional

5. Higher Moving

4. Instinctive

3. Intellectual

2. Emotional

1. Moving

The Instinctive Center

The instinctive center is a key to your entire energetic system. It contains all information related to survival needed to keep your body alive. However it also stores all information related to unfinished business and lessons from other lifetimes. Knowing how your instinctive center is structured and how it functions is the key to understanding all your self-karma and the karmic ribbons that hold you in constant imbalance.

Your life plan consisting of your overleaves, life task, self-karma, karma, and astrological makeup determines how your instinctive center is organized each lifetime. It is set up according to relevant survival information from past lives and earlier events this lifetime, all by association.

In addition your instinctive center is divided into three parts; the intellectual part consisting of its reasoning and its associations; the emotional part, consisting of fears and intense emotions related to survival; and the moving part, consisting of impulses to fight, meet, or flee karma or danger.

You have learned the key steps in working to balance disharmonies in your instinctive center. You have also learned the relevance of breathing to working with your instinctive center.

Each twelve and twenty five years you get the opportunity to automatically review your instinctive center. If you resist, you pile up imbalance over lifetimes until you force yourself to have an instinctively centered lifetime. That ensures that you will ultimately face and experience unfinished lessons that you have avoided or resisted. When you have let things get so far out of hand, you set up conditions for extreme emotional imbalance and mental illness. The healing of them is often the living of them through.

GOALS AND MODES AS VEHICLES OF HEALING.

Resistance to your life goal is perhaps the greatest cause of imbalance that you can find. When you fight your primary motivator in life you end up operating out of your chief feature and the negative poles of your overleaves in general. This causes imbalance on every level of your personality. eventually this can result in physical illness and disease as well.

Next to goals, modes can produce the most imbalance if expressed negatively. Recall that your mode is your primary method or style. It is the way you approach your goal. When you operate out of the negative pole of your mode, you set conditions up for extreme disharmony.

Both expressing your goal and your mode through the negative poles creates conditions of excessive stress in the body. Eventually the body succumbs to viral infections, ulcers, cancers, and the like unless the positive poles are accessed.

You can use your goal and your mode to get you out of disharmony by deliberately and consciously working toward expressing them in the positive poles. Of course just knowing what your goal and your mode is can be extraordinarily helpful.

So, there you have it. Moving toward the positive poles of all your overleaves and eliminating the influence of your chief feature is ultimately healing. As you do so you move yourself out of self karma and you stop creating the imbalance of karma. You begin to repay your existing karma in ways that are more creative and releasing. You can begin to experience the joy of life and the wonder of the great game that you helped the Tao to create. You get closer to celebrating that party the Tao has been preparing for your return. You can even start celebrating now because the Tao doesn't care about what time it is.

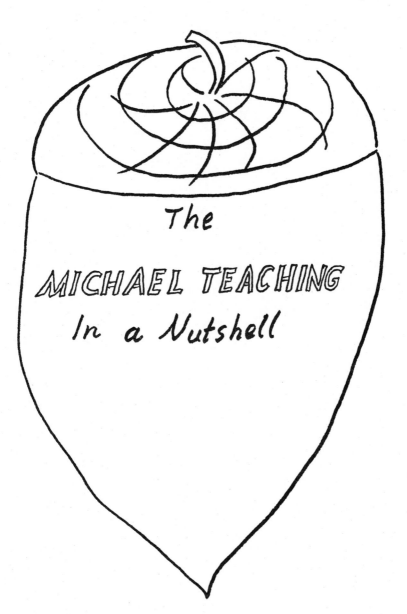

The

MICHAEL TEACHING
In a Nutshell

Appendix

The Michael Teaching—A Summary

This section is a brief review of basic knowledge presented in The Michael Handbook *(formerly* Essence and Personality*). It is foundation material and will be most helpful in understanding the information in this book about relationships.*

Michael is a teacher from the causal plane who offers this body of knowledge freely and unconditionally in order to assist people to understand themselves and one another better. According to Michael this teaching is an ancient one that is occasionally updated to keep up with changes in language and culture.

Michael is a reunited entity who lived many lives on the earth before cycling off to other planes and experiences. Michael draws their name from the last life of their last fragment to live on the Earth. Michael's teaching has come through a variety of trance mediums and channels over the last twenty years and continues to do so.

Michael is available and willing to channel through anyone who is interested in this material. Michael suggests that all the information be self-validated and thrown out if it does not strike a chord with you.

This teaching represents an evolution of the works of Gurdjieff, Ouspensky, and Rodney Collin who began to bring forth this knowledge earlier this century.

According to the Michael entity, life is an exciting game of learning set up by the Tao (all that is) for purposes of creativity and pure expression. The physical plane, the seventh and most solid plane, is the dimension of forgetfulness and separation. Here the Tao is pretending not to know itself in a cosmic game of hide and seek. The goal is to find oneness and wholeness through a series of experiences and lifetimes where lessons are learned about unconditional acceptance of self and others.

Entities seeking to experience this grand adventure fragment themselves into hundreds of individuals who progress and develop through a series of lifetimes. Through their many chosen personalities these fragment essences gradually discover their essential oneness and eventually reunite with one another. They continue for further adventures in the six remaining planes enroute to final joyful unity with the Tao itself.

The fragment essences progress through seven distinct stages of development, each with seven levels apiece. Each stage is distinguished by a unique level of perception and by particular characteristics. Here then are the major soul ages passed through by each fragment.

Infant Soul

This is a beginning level of survival and an orientation to the physical human form. Infant souls are instinctively fearful and seek out extremes of experience in order to become acquainted with physical life. They experience life in a "me and not me" format and they approach their world superstitiously. Infant souls learn by rote and seek guidance from older, more experienced souls. They do not question nor philosophize, preferring to follow absolutely the authority of their leader. Infant souls are overwhelmed by complex urban society and prefer to learn basic rules of living in small tribal and out-of-the-way environments.

Baby Soul

The baby soul has become acquainted with the basics of living and now becomes focused on developing rules and structures for the building of society. As such, baby souls are oriented toward law and order, preferring to further develop their conscience through experiences that test the social rules they themselves have made.

Life for the baby soul is perceived in a "me and other me's" format. They seek and honor absolute higher authority to provide a meaningful context for living. Their religions are dogmatic and orthodox to the extreme. Tradition plays an important role in life of the baby soul and the breaking of tradition meets with dire consequences.

Khomeini of Iran is a Baby soul.

Young Soul

Young souls have become sophisticated and are highly enthusiastic about playing the material game. They seek power, notoriety, fame, fortune, and wealth. They aspire to the heights of human achievement in sports, campaigns, competitions, and academics. The perceptivity of the young soul is that of "me and you and I'm going to win." The young soul is predominantly focused on looking good and making it to the top of of the heap.

Young souls begin to reflect on their actions and question who they are in the final levels. However they are usually too focused on the maya of external events to achieve much self understanding. Alexander the Great was a young soul as was Cleopatra.

Mature Soul

The mature soul age is the adolescence of soul levels. Here dramatic changes occur in perception and overall awareness. The mature soul turns inward and reflects on his own awareness. Philosophy and the beginning of true spiritual awareness are the result. The perceptivity of the mature soul is "you and I are alike, I know how you feel inside." This represents the relaxing of psychic boundaries and at times the breakdown of personality. Highly emotional, the mature soul focuses on intensity and duration in relationship with others.

Mature souls seek peace and quiet and turn away from organized religion to find their guidance. Often feeling misunderstood and out of step with their cultures, they prefer to be with older souls for understanding and support. Even so they often make major contributions to human knowledge and understanding. Galileo was a mature soul as well as Fritz Perls.

Old Soul

The old soul is a contradiction in terms. Laid back, casual, and ofttimes lazy, the old soul accelerates the pace of spiritual search. You can imagine the intense inner activity of an older person who is no longer active in pursuing achievement but rather is focused on preparing for death.

Old souls are sensual, independent, and usually highly eccentric. They are capable and wise, often eschewing traditional forms of education in favor of their own form of study. They perceive the world as "you and I as part of something greater." John Muir was an old soul.

Transcendental Soul

When all the entity fragments have cycled off the physical plane at the end of their old soul cycle they reunite together again, enriched and expanded beyond measure. They may choose to incarnate in human form one more time as a group and not fragmented. This incarnation is called the transcendental soul or Bodhisattva, the helping soul who is recognized as a great spiritual teacher by older souls. Mohandas Ghandi was one.

Infinite Soul

The infinite soul is a representative of the Tao itself. The infinite soul takes human form very occasionally to provide leadership in times of chaos and distress. Buddha, Christ, Krishna, and Lao Tsu were the infinite soul manifested.

THE SEVEN LEVELS WITHIN EACH SOUL AGE

As mentioned, each soul age has seven levels of learning. These levels are progressive and and require at least one, if not several lifetimes to complete. The same set of seven applies to each soul age.

The Seven Levels within each Soul Age

1. Examine new soul age —explore
2. Transition/creation —self-karma: plunge in
3. Introspection —adapt to change internally
4. Emotions —exemplifies stage
5. New knowledge —eccentricity
6. Karmic completion —intense and busy life
7. Teaching —share, consolidate, and prepare for next stage.

THE ESSENCE ROLE

Essence chooses one of seven roles to develop and master during its journey from infant soul to old soul perception. This role remains the same throughout the cycle of lifetimes and represents a particular approach to living that shall here be described. The seven roles are divided into four main categories or axes: inspiration, expression, action, and assimilation.

Servers and Priests

Under the inspiration classification is the ordinal role of server and the exalted role of priest. Servers comprise 30% of the population and derive profound satisfaction in being of service to others in a direct and immediate fashion. Priests on the other hand represent only 4% of the population and they seek to serve larger groups by providing spiritual guidance.

Artisans and Sages

The expression roles are the ordinal role of artisan, 20% of the population, and the exalted role of sage, 15% of the population. Artisans strive to express themselves through creativity of a direct and personal nature. Sages express themselves to larger groups through drama, communication and amusement.

Warriors and Kings

The action roles are the ordinal role of warrior, 20% of the population, and the exalted king role, only 1% of the population. Warriors are the most physical of the roles and enjoy lives of direct and confrontive experience in the physical world. They are productive and good at finding strategic ways of achieving their logically thought-out goals. Kings prefer to delegate the action to others and lead through their grandeur and sense of responsibility for the group.

Scholars

The scholar, 10% of the population, is the assimilative role and is primarily neutral. Scholars seek to experience life through the accumulation of knowledge and spend many lives researching and studying what is around them. They understand all the other roles and act as mediators between them.

OVERLEAVES

Essence has developed a personality, gradually formed over many lifetimes, and this larger personality expresses itself through the more limited personality adopted for each lifetime.

When essence takes physical form through birth in a human body, it chooses and develops this temporary personality by giving itself the proper life conditions to develop specific traits called overleaves. The negative expression of this limited and temporary personality is called the false personality. The task for each lifetime is to dissolve the false personality and express the true personality through the overleaves chosen.

Although the role remains the same throughout the cycle of lives, each lifetime the soul selects a new goal, attitude, chief feature, mode, center, and body type. This gives the individual a new personality to work with and provides a fresh and contrasting range of opportunities and challenges.

GOALS

The goal orients and motivates you to seek out certain life experiences. The seven goals available to choose from are re-evaluation, growth, discrimination, acceptance, submission, dominance, and stagnation.

Re-evaluation motivates you to take a closer look at yourself and is sometimes accompanied by a severe physical disability. Growth is the motivation to experience as much as possible in a given lifetime. These are usually full and busy lives. Discrimination leads you to reject all of the chaff in life and to retain only that which is considered best. Acceptance on the other hand leads you to accept life as it comes.

Submission teaches you to surrender to a teacher, cause, or a life's work. Dominance is the desire to lead and to command. Stagnation is the motivation to make life flow easily and is usually a lifetime for rest.

All goals are eventually chosen and mastered throughout the cycle of lives.

ATTITUDES

The attitude gives you a habitual point of view. There are seven attitudes to choose from: stoic, spiritualist, skeptic, idealist, cynic, realist, and pragmatist.

Stoics reserve judgment while spiritualists tend to see the overall picture about what can be.

Skeptics doubt and investigate and idealists strive for progress by seeing what should or ought to be.

Cynics readily see what won't work while realists see all the possibilities at once.

Pragmatists are efficient and want things to work.

All the attitudes are eventually selected and mastered.

CHIEF NEGATIVE OBSTACLE

In addition to the goal and attitude, each fragment selects from among seven chief negative obstacles. These act as impediments to be overcome and tend to neutralize efforts to attain the goal. The seven obstacles are self-deprecation, arrogance, self-destruction, greed, martyrdom, impatience, and stubbornness.

Self-deprecation refers to a pervasive sense of low self-esteem, while arrogance hides an uncomfortable shyness resulting from a fear of vulnerability.

Self-destruction results in slow or rapid suicide. Greed comes from the fear that not enough of anything is available.

Martyrdom is feeling a victim of circumstances. Impatience is the fear of missing out.

Stubbornness can impede through obstinacy and represents a fear of change.

MODE

The mode is the means of achieving the goal. The seven modes that can be chosen are reserve, passion, caution, power, perseverance, aggression, and observation.

Reserve appears restrained while passion is unbridled and expansive, identified with life's drama.

Caution appears tentative, while power mode appears authoritative and in control.

Perseverance makes one appear disciplined or repetitive.

Aggression leads one to impose oneself on the world.

Observation is a common mode and facilitates learning by careful watching.

All modes are eventually embraced and mastered.

CENTERS

Seven centers give a person even more alternatives to choose from each lifetime. The three centers that are predominantly chosen for everyday functioning are moving center, intellectual center, and emotional center.

These centers act as primary energizers and determine the way that a person generally responds to any stimuli.

A moving centered person will tend to be physically active and be fond of sports, travel, and action. An emotionally centered person will tend to be more perceptive and will experience situations in terms of likes and dislikes.

An intellectually centered person will tend to be more verbal and will enjoy philosophy and thinking for its own sake.

The instinctive center stores survival information and is operative in everyone all the time.

The higher centers—higher moving, higher intellectual, and higher emotional—are transformational states of awareness achieved during peak experiences or in meditation states. They are always available but seldom accessed by most people.

BODY TYPES

There are seven major bodytypes to choose from, determined by the configuration of planets at the time of your conception. These are Solar, Mars, Venus, Saturn, Lunar, Mercury, and Jupiter. The planetary types influence physical characteristics as well as personality style. Most people are a combination of three planetary influences. Three additional planets, Uranus, Neptune, and Pluto, are more rare influences.

Solar is bright, elfish, and refined.
Mars is muscular, reddish, and vigorous.
Venus is voluptuous, warm, and passive.
Saturn is tall, rugged, and enduring.
Lunar is round, pale, and luminous.
Mercury is active, bright, and versatile.
Jupiter is grand, fleshy, and broad.
Uranus is eccentric.
Neptune is dreamy.
Pluto is far-reaching.

SUMMARY

This section has summarized the basics of the Michael teaching's perspective on life purpose and orientation. Here the focus has been on Michael's comprehensive system for understanding the fundamentals of personality and the uniqueness of each individual character structure. Accordingly, the uniqueness of a personality comes from the particular blend of traits chosen; the role, the stage of soul development, and the nature of accumulated past life experiences.

Remember that the fragment essence must pass through seven main stages of development, each with seven levels of growth. These stages and levels are specific, progressive, and characterized by particular lessons. Each lifetime a set of personality traits and a life purpose is selected for the role to master. Each of these traits or overleaves has a positive and a negative pole. Being in the negative pole creates disharmony and neurosis while being in the positive pole creates satisfaction and health. The older the soul, the greater facility in moving toward positive poles via understanding and self-awareness.

The overall goal is for each fragment to experience all of life and progress toward wholeness, integration, and balance through self-acceptance and agape.

A much more thorough and detailed presentation of soul ages, levels, and overleaves may be found in the book *A Michael Handbook* (formerly *Essence and Personality*) from Warwick Press, Orinda California, 1987.

Glossary

agape	Unconditional love.
agreement	An arrangement between two fragments.
aspect	A parallel self in a parallel universe.
astrology	Configuration of planets at birth influencing life plan.
attitude	Primary perspective.
audacity	Daring or bold move.
basic plan	General design for a lifetime.
being	Unit of intelligent consciousness sparked from the Tao.
belief	Trust without verification.
bird	Fifth major area of exploration for beings considering human form. Includes many simple mammals as well.
body type	Structure of body determined by astrological influences.

cadence	Set of seven fragments of which you are part. Your number within this group of seven influences.
cadre	Group of seven entities with whom you interact most lifetimes. There are about 7000 fragments in a cadre.
center	Overleaf that determines your primary reaction to any life situation. Vehicle of communication between essence and personality.
—higher center	Essence perception.
—lower center	Personality perception.
chakra	Vortex of energy principally located along the spinal column. Associated with the centers. Communication and energy distribution point.
channel	To receive and disseminate information and communication from non-physical planes.
chief feature	Principal obstacle to achieving your goal in a lifetime.
circuit	Completion of all seven roles in seven series of lifetimes.
coalescence	Coming together. Making possible.
coercion	The use of force to achieve an objective.
concentration	A form of spiritual practice that includes focusing the mind on specifics. Visualization and affirmations.
contingent	7000 cadres or 49 million fragments. One percent of the earth's population.
contradiction	To give opposing views or beliefs.
cord	Energetic connection between two people in order to communicate or draw energy. Specifically between their chakras.

cycle	A complete set of lifetimes from infant to old soul stages from the perspective of one role.
death	Seventh internal monad; facilitates much karma.
degree of essence	Level of knowing the Tao. There are seven degrees, ranging from limited to all-inclusive perception.
deva	Astral plane being that tends and assists oceans, minerals, plants, and animals. They gradually develop toward sentience.
ego	False personality. Dies with physical body.
energy	Action component of universe.
enlightenment	The experience of knowing the truth, love, and energy of the Tao.
entity	Your family of consciousness; oversoul; 800 to 1200 fragments. Comprised of several essences.
—fragment	A single member of an entity. Membership in an essence.
essence	Soul. Intermediary between the Tao and the fragment personality each lifetime. Comprised of a number of fragments. Several essences comprise an entity.
—twin	Soulmate. A fragment who parallels your lifetimes. An intense relationship with the fragment that understands you the most. You each reflect each other's overleaves and essence role.
—mate	Essence twin from a past cycle, a relationship of affinity.
exalted	Wide focus, visionary.
false personality	Behavior stemming from negative poles of overleaves, the chief feature, and imprinting.

frequency	Vibration rate of an essence or role.
gemstone	Minerals that intensify or reduce the effect of your overleaves when you wear them or are near them.
goal	Primary motivator each lifetime. Major overleaf.
God	Tao, Great Spirit, Atman, Supreme Being, All That Is.
Gurdjieff, G.	Armenian teacher who laid the foundations for the Michael teachings earlier in this century.
heart link	One with whom you have a special loving relationship resulting from many lifetimes of experience together.
identification	Loss of individuality without understanding. Taking on another's problems.
illusion	Maya, forgetfulness, belief in the physical plane appearance of things only.
imprinting	Conditioning, programming, hypnosis. Taking on another's way of seeing or doing things without conscious awareness.
insect	Third area of exploration for beings considering human form.
instinctive	Survival oriented reactions.
—center	Your memory banks of all past life and present life survival information.
—review	A look at recent past experience to help plan the next step.
integration	Putting together essence and personality for balance and harmony.

internal monad	There are seven. Rite of passage within a single lifetime that allows you to continue to the next level of growth. Includes birth, puberty, maturity, death.
karma	Universal law of consequences or balance; caused by interfering with or promoting another's free choice. Seen as positive or negative on the physical plane. Based on triadic processes.
ladder	See nontet.
love	Feeling or experience of oneness. First position of quadrant that gets ideas.
mammal	Sixth major area of exploration in devic form for beings considering sentience.
maya	Illusion, self deception, looking real but not so.
meditation	A form of spiritual exercise. Emptying the mind of all thought forms.
Michael	Causal plane reunited entity comprised of kings and warriors; non-physical author of this book.
mineral	First major area of exploration for a being coming to the planet. Includes all global experiences explored in devic form.
mode	Your primary method of doing things each lifetime; a major overleaf.
monad	A unit of life experience; must be experienced from both sides in order to complete the reincarnational cycle.
nontet	A group of nine, oriented to the success of a single goal.

octave	A stable group of eight made up of two quadrants.
	A complete cycle of learning that leads to the next level of growth.
order of casting	The position that you hold within your . entity
ordinal	Narrowly focused; oriented toward immediacy and one-to-one interactions with others.
Ouspensky, P.D.	Student and essence twin of Gurdjieff. Put early versions of this teaching into writing.
overleaves	Specific traits and characteristics that make up personality each lifetime. Goal, mode, attitude, chief feature, centering, and body type.
pentangle	Unstable group of five. Usually dedicated to fulfillment of a spiritual task.
personality	Made up of overleaves and imprinting each lifetime; unique flavor or style of being.
—essence personality	Unique style of being, made up of role, cadence, casting number, entity membership, and experiences from accumulated lifetimes.
plane	Seven relative levels of experience created by the Tao for evolutionary purposes. Physical, Astral, Causal, Akashic, Mental, Messianic, Buddhaic.
—physical	Most solid, slow, forgetful of all planes offering the experience of separateness.
plant	Third area of exploration in devic form for a being considering human form.
pole	Extremes of overleaves, either positive or negative.
—positive	Essence oriented function of overleaf.

—negative	False personality function of overleaf.
power animal	Source of guidance and information. The sum total of all knowledge of one species of animal.
prosperity	Experience of abundance in health, spirituality, love, truth, etc.
quadrant	A stable group of four people, oriented toward fulfilling tasks.
reptile	Includes fish. Fourth major exploration area in devic form for beings considering sentience.
role	Primary beingness through which a fragment experiences all of life.
self-karma	Lessons that you give yourself that involve the extremes of an experience, such as rich-poor, happy-sad, healthy-sick. Also something that you either hate about yourself or are excessively vain about.
sentient	Ensouled; having intellectual part of intellectual center developed; having self-awareness.
septant	A group of seven people oriented toward visionary or special projects. An evolutionary growth pattern comprising seven steps. Leads to an octave.
service	A form of spiritual exercise that includes helping others.
sextant	A stable group of six people oriented toward the fulfillment of life tasks. Made up of two triads.
sexual	Combining male and female energies; can be physical or energetic as in the higher planes.
soul age	Development of perceptivity on a continuum from infant soul to old soul level.

—level	There are seven levels within each soul age. Each embodies a special set of lessons and experiences.
spirit	Essence and personality are contained within it.
spiritual	Awake and aware; state of remembering the Tao.
spirit guide	Assistant, healer, guide from a non-physical plane. Often a member of your own entity.
support circle	Twelve specific positions of assistance filled by family and friends.
Tao	All That Is, Great Spirit, God, Atman.
task companion	A special person chosen at the beginning of the cycle with whom you do life tasks.
teaching	A spiritual path that has the potential to guide you closer to the Tao.
triad	A group of three; also a process and unit of learning. Creates intensity and karma; subdivision of a septant; Law of Three.
truth	What is. Also relative to you, your perspective in the Tao.
universe	A sequence, complete in its entirety, of all the stars, planets, structures and beings of one of the Tao's creations. There are an infinite number of universes.
—parallel	A new universe created for every significant possible outcome of a given event.
wakefulness	Knowing or remembering the Tao; prerequisite to spiritual growth.
walk-in	One essence agrees to take over the body that another essence is leaving without death ensuing. Overleaves and role may completely change.

OVERLEAF CHART

| | EXPRESSION | | INSPIRATION | | ACTION | | ASSIMILATION |
	Ordinal	Exalted	Ordinal	Exalted	Ordinal	Exalted	Neutral
ROLE	+Creation ARTISAN -Self-Deception	+Dissemination SAGE -Verbosity	+Service SERVER -Bondage	+Compassion PRIEST -Zeal	+Persuasion WARRIOR -Coercion	+Mastery KING -Tyranny	+Knowledge SCHOLAR -Theory
GOAL	+Sophistication DISCRIMINATION -Rejection	+Agape ACCEPTANCE -Ingratiation	+Simplicity RE-EVALUATION -Withdrawal	+Evolution GROWTH -Confusion	+Devotion SUBMISSION -Exploited	+Leadership DOMINANCE -Dictatorship	+Free-Flowing STAGNATION -Inertia
ATTITUDE	+Investigation SKEPTIC -Suspicion	+Coalescence IDEALIST -Naivety	+Tranquility STOIC -Resignation	+Verification SPIRITUALIST -Beliefs	+Contradiction CYNIC -Denigration	+Objective REALIST -Subjective	+Practical PRAGMATIST -Dogmatic
CHIEF FEATURE	+Sacrifice SELF-DESTRUCTION -Suicidal	+Appetite GREED Voracity	+Humility SELF-DEPRECATION -Abasement	+Pride ARROGANCE -Vanity	+Selflessness MARTYRDOM -Victimization	+Daring IMPATIENCE -Intolerance	+Determination STUBBORNNESS -Obstinacy
MODE	+Deliberation CAUTION -Phobia	+Authority POWER -Oppression	+Restraint RESERVED -Inhibition	+Self-Actualization PASSION -Identification	+Persistence PERSEVERANCE -Unchanging	+Dynamism AGGRESSION -Belligerence	+Clarity OBSERVATION -Surveillance
CENTER	+Insight INTELLECTUAL -Reasoning	+Truth HIGHER INTELLECTUAL -Telepathy	+Perception EMOTIONAL -Sentimentality	+Love HIGHER EMOTIONAL -Intuition	+Productive MOVING -Frenetic	+Integration HIGHER MOVING -Desire	+Aware INSTINCTIVE -Mechanical
BODY TYPES	+Grandeur JUPITER -Overwhelming	+Agile MERCURY -Nervous	+Luminous LUNAR -Pallid	+Rugged SATURN -Gaunt	+Voluptuous VENUS -Sloppy	+Wiry MARS -Impulsive	+Radiant SOLAR -Ethereal

New Michael Books

Available through your bookseller or from Affinity Press.

The Michael Handbook
formerly *Essence and Personality: The Michael Handbook*
by Jose Stevens, Ph.D, and Simon Warwick-Smith
This 350 page reference book entertains you while you learn. It
covers the grand scheme, soul ages and levels, roles, overleaves,
centering, body types, the planetary shift and more—in depth.
Also, a guide to help you find your overleaves.
$12.95, Affinity Press.

Tao to Earth: Michael's Guide to Relationships and Growth
by Jose Stevens, Ph.D.
This fully illustrated, informative book is a practical and
entertaining guide to such diverse topics as understanding
intimate relationships, how the laws of karma work and the
nature of prosperity. Included is a review of the basics of the
Michael Teaching for new readers.
$11.95, Affinity Press.

The World According to Michael: An Old Soul's Guide to the
Universe
by Joya Pope
A delightful and succinct "sage's" romp through the basics of the
Michael teaching—lots of information in a small, fun-to -read
package. For friends who are curious, it's a starter book of choice.
$8.95, Sage Publications.

Michael: The Basic Teachings
by Aaron Christeaan, J.P. Van Hulle and M.C. Clark
Just what the title says, an overview of the basics; overleaves,
relationships, etc.
$11.95, Affinity Press.

Michael's Gemstone Dictionary
by Judithann David, Ph.D., channeled by J.P. Van Hulle
Energies and uses of gems and minerals according to the Michael
teaching. Hundreds of precious and semi-precious gems for
memory, money, imagination, well being, etc. Find out why
you're attracted to your favorite stones. Fascinating and useful.
$8.95, Affinity Press.

By Jose and Lena Stevens
*The Secrets of Shamanism: Tapping the Spirit Power Within
You*
$3.95, Avon Books.

Resources

Reprints of the Essence and Personality Questionnaire from *The
Personality Puzzle* can be obtained from Pivot Press, Please call
(415) 845-5725. $2.50 for one, $50. for 25, $175. for 100. Call or
write for larger orders. Postage $.50 for one, $1.00 for 50, $2.00 for
100. In California please add 7% tax.

Books may be ordered from Affinity Press, 2 Austin Court,
Orinda, California, 94563. Please add $1.00 per book for postage
and handling. In California, please add 7% tax.

About the Author

Jose Stevens, Ph.D is a writer and licensed psychotherapist in Berkeley, California. He obtained his masters degree at the University of California at Berkeley and his doctorate at the California Institute of Integral Studies in San Francisco. Currently he teaches in the Department for the Study of Consciousness at John F. Kennedy University and lectures widely on Essence and Personality, shamanism, and prosperity. He is the founder of Essence Psychology, a non-pathological perspective on personality. For information regarding workshops, consultation, channeling, and intuition trainings, write to him at P.O. Box 5314, Berkeley, California, 94705.

Keep In Contact
with
The Michael Community
Subscribe *NOW* to
THE MICHAEL CONNECTION

- Featuring all the latest information about the Michael Teaching
- Focusing each issue on the basics of the Michael Teaching
- Resource directory for Michael teachers in the Bay Area
- Periodic reports from the Michael Community nationwide
- Articles of general interest to Michael students and all others in the metaphysical community
- Pictures, poetry, gossip, personal ads and much, much more...

The Michael Connection exists to support those who wish to use
The Michael Teaching to become more effective players
in the game of life.

Join us and connect.

**Fill this out and mail to: The Michael Connection
P.O. Box 1873, Orinda, CA 94563**

- -

☐ **Subscription.** Mail the next 4 issues (1 year) to me at the address below for only $15. (Outside U.S. $20.00)

☐ **Back Issues.** Send me back issues featuring the following roles (Circle each you wish to have sent):
Warriors Artisans Servers Scholars Sages Priests Kings
I have enclosed $4 for each issue.*

☐ Send me information about other available back issues.

☐ **Advertising.** I'd love to enjoy patronage from the Michael community.

ne:_____ Phone:_____

ess: _____

/State/Zip: _____

Please make checks payable to: The Michael Connection
issue is sold out, a photocopy of the issue will be substituted. Please let us know if
prefer NOT to receive a photocopy